MADDOCK, Brent. The films of Jacques Tati. Scarecrow, 1977. 179p ill bibl filmography index 77-11084. 7.00 ISBN 0-8108-1065-4. C.I.P.

This book is a thorough illumination of the phenomenon of Jacques Tati, the remarkable French comic film actor and director. Tati is both the subject of a film cult and the clown idol of millions who adore particularly his early films, *Les vacances de Monsieur* (1953) and *Mon oncle* (1958). Surprisingly, Tati has written, directed, and starred in only five major feature films, and none of these is widely shown. Maddock carefully and admiringly leads the reader through Tati's brilliant creation of M. Hulot and the magnificent movies Hulot inhabits. He places Tati within the context of other great visual comedians (Chaplin, Keaton, et al.), discusses and reviews each feature film, and concludes with reflections on Tati's "universe" and comedy style. This is the fullest examination available of Tati's comic genius. The accompanying photographs were carefully selected.

The Films of
Jacques Tati

by

Brent Maddock

The Scarecrow Press, Inc.
Metuchen, N.J. & London
1977

Acknowledgments:

Dr. Joseph A. Casper (U.S.C. Dept. of Cinema),
Richard Fernandez, Patrick Roth and Kirk Maddock

Frontispiece:

Jacques Tati in the 1970's
(Courtesy French Film Office)

Use has been made in this
work of certain passages
from Jonathan Rosenbaum's
"Tati's Democracy," Film
Comment vol. 9, no. 3
(May/June 1973), copyright©
1973 by Film Comment Pub-
lishing Corporation, and re-
printed by permission of the
Film Society of Lincoln Center.

Library of Congress Cataloging in Publication Data

Maddock, Brent, 1950-
    The films of Jacques Tati.

    Bibliography: p.
    Filmography: p.
    Includes index.
    1. Tati, Jacques. I. Title.
PN1998.A3T335   791.43'028'0924 [B]   77-11084
ISBN 0-8108-1065-4

To My
Mother and Father,
With Love

CONTENTS

"... he is a scatter-brained angel and the disorder he produces is that of tenderness and of liberty."

> --André Bazin, Que-est-ce que
> le Cinéma? Volume I.

CHAPTER 1

AN INTRODUCTION:
TATI AND HIS TIME

It seems a bit unfair for the first two decades of film comedy to have provided the major works of Chaplin, Keaton and Lloyd. Fifty and sixty years after the fact, film clowns still scurry about in pursuit of the gifts these men had to offer. The impact of these early film comedies was so great that all film comedy since not only owes a debt to these pioneers but is, either openly or unconsciously, held up to their high standards. If one truly appreciates the work of the great silent clowns, how far can one abandon oneself to the comedy of their numerous imitators?

If Chaplin, Keaton and Lloyd (ironically the names have begun to solidify into a single term with a single meaning) searched for archetypal film characters, then today's clowns are simply imitating these already unearthed archetypes, sometimes obviously and sometimes couched in disguise. It might have been much easier for film comedy had it been given a chance, over a longer period of time, to work its way up to the level of the early comedy masters; if years of film experience were needed to develop a Chaplin or a Keaton. To have been given these great artists so early in film's history only causes filmmakers to gaze fondly and a bit forlornly backwards.

The question that naturally arises is: "Can anyone bring the genius of early film comedy to bear in a contemporary film?" Would it not be possible, in addition, to create a new comedy archetype? As the conditions of life in early twentieth century America were able to produce the worldly but sentimental tramp and the eternally resourceful "great stoneface," so might the rapidly changing lifestyles of the mid-century Western world produce its own comedy archetype. What is required is a filmmaker who straddles the

1

gap between old and new; who brings that early manifested
genius to play amongst the landscape of today. This book
proposes that the French comedy filmmaker Jacques Tati has
succeeded more than any other contemporary filmmaker in
doing just this. Tati, like his predecessors Chaplin and
Keaton and unlike most movie funnymen, is a clown, that is,
a character with an essential or metaphysical base, deriving
his comedy talents from outside contemporary or relative
ideas of what is funny. Tati's filmic persona is Monsieur
Hulot, a character with as universal a basis as Chaplin's
tramp.

Tati holds an odd place in the critic's eye view of the
film world. He is, at the same time, both the most contemporary of filmmakers, dealing with subject matter that
could only be found at this juncture of history, and the most
classic of filmmakers, using a technical style and filmic
structure close to early silent comedies. These contradic-
tions make it difficult to categorize Tati, to draw easy comparisons, to place him in a broader context and to do all
else that a film historian finds necessary.

In addition, Tati's output has been less than prolific.
At the well seasoned age of sixty-nine he has written, directed and starred in only five feature films, with a sixth
on the drawing board. Tati's meticulous style of production,
not unlike the feature work of Griffith or Chaplin or the contemporary Kubrick, has made his films more a rare specialty than a reflection of any current trends. The release of
a new Tati film is looked upon as an event. Unfortunately,
in the U.S. it is but a small group of extremely loyal fans
that awaits Tati's next feature. It becomes necessary, with
each new release, for a large portion of Tati's audience to
discover him as something brand new. As Tati has often
explained his meager output to enthusiastic fans: "If we remain faithful to one line of conduct don't we have enough
things to recount in our lives. I hate to repeat myself."[1]*

Tati's five feature films to date are: Jour de Fête
(1949), Les Vacances de Monsieur Hulot (1953), Mon Oncle
(1958), Playtime (1967) and, in the correct French spelling,
Trafic (1971). Throughout this more than twenty years' span
of films runs Tati's recurrent themes of the human spirit
versus the technological regimentation of modern life. What

---

*See Chapter Notes, beginning on page 165.

Jacques Tati (courtesy French Film Office).

characterizes Tati's films even more than his choice of
themes is his unique filmic style. A Tati film is an odd
combination of silent and sound film, of old-style sight gags
in contemporary settings and of loose story structure with
contemporary subject matter. Tati is able, more successfully than any contemporary comedy filmmaker, to construct
his own filmic universe using a delicate balance between
comic situations, sound effects, characterizations, settings,
screen size and pacing. That Tati is able to build his own
universe, a universe where the human voice is used as just
one of the infinite number of expressive sound effects; where
characters behave in exaggerations of the patterns that everyone lives by, and that he is able to overcome our uncon-
scious expectation of characters who speak and act in a certain prescribed way--all of this is an indication of his control and of his vision.

        Tati's simplicity of story structure sets him apart
from other filmmakers. He has no pretensions to any elaborate plot devices in order to present his gags. There are

those, like Stanley Kauffmann, who have felt Tati's singleness
of purpose should be put to better use:

> I always feel a little guilty about Jacques Tati. The
> man has so much of what one is always bemoaning
> the shortage of: taste, skill, personal vision. Yet
> his films leave me with something of the feeling I
> get from a Marcel Marceau performance--technique
> and talent employed in the pursuit of preciosity. [2]

There has not been, however, a better practitioner of
the visual gag than Tati. No excuses are necessary when comparing him with any one of the early masters. If Kauffmann
finds Tati's work lacking substance and a certain dimension, it
must be realized that Tati's films are not so much stories or
character studies as they are explorations of the systems and
structures that make up society: architecture, transportation,
the home, time-saving appliances and the vacation, for example. Tati chooses to explore the physical and cultural environment of which he has found himself a part. He will leap
freely from subject to subject as his curiosity dictates. He
will hover over certain areas and return to others that he
feels warrant closer examination.

In doing research on Jacques Tati, one finds that the
simple mention of his name produces one of two responses: a
blank stare or a knowledgeable smile. As Basil Wright has
accurately observed, "Tati is a rare bird; the mere mention
of his films is liable to start people off in a laughing fit. "[3]

It is Tati's quality of independence and absolute fidelity
to his personal vision that allows him to play such a unique
role in the cinema. Penelope Houston, writing in Sight and
Sound, observed as far back as 1959 that something placed Tati
apart from his contemporaries:

> It is a long time ... since the cinema encouraged
> audacity in its artists.... Most current screen
> comedies are content to set up their neat little tar-
> gets ... retire to a safe distance and pepper them
> with small arms fire. Since Chaplin abdicated ...
> there has been no one who has made comedies be-
> cause he could do nothing else--no one, that is, ex-
> cept Jacques Tati. [4]

Tati serves us all by refusing to cash in his perceptions for
that which an audience might more easily understand and as-

similate. As Tati has simply stated: "I have likened myself
to a painter. I may not be great but I paint what I like."[5]

* * * *

It seems impossible to assign Tati to any school of
filmmaking. One keeps comparing his works to the films of
an era that had passed before he ever started making films.
He fits and yet he does not. There has also been very little written on Tati's works. Magazine articles appear in
clumps, corresponding to the release of his latest film. Outside of these the shelves are nearly bare when it comes to
Tati. Armand J. Cauliez has written and compiled the most
substantial volume on criticism of the filmmaker. Available
only in French, Cauliez's Jacques Tati examines the influences
on Tati from his earliest short subjects up through his fourth
feature, Playtime. Cauliez has also compiled essays on Tati
from a wide variety of French critics. Geneviève Agel's
Hulot Parmi Nous (Hulot Among Us) is a slim volume of criticism on Tati's first two feature films with explorations of
Tati's mime background and his creation of the Hulot character. This book, also, is available only in French.

Available in English are novelized versions of both
Les Vacances de Monsieur Hulot and Mon Oncle. Written by
Jean-Claud Carrière and illustrated by Pierre Etaix, the books
take on a very charming storybook quality. Penelope Gilliatt's
New Yorker profile of Tati, written shortly after the release
of Trafic, is one of the most insightful and personal studies of
both the man and his films. Jonathan Rosenbaum's Film Comment article, "Tati's Democracy," is another solid contribution
to the existing literature on Tati. Rosenbaum analyzes the
very structures of Playtime to define the conscious use of line,
movement and framing. Finally, André Bazin's and François
Truffaut's "Entretien avec Jacques Tati" ("Conversation with
Tati") in Cahiers du Cinéma is about the best interview one
can find on Tati's films up to and including Mon Oncle. The
filmgoing public, naturally, seems more interested in this year's
celebrity director than in a filmmaker whose contribution can
best be felt by surveying the work of the past two and a half
decades.

Tati is a filmmaker who is directly a product of the
era in which he lives. He deals with the universe of social
customs, industrialization, transportation and the spider web
of progress in which one, in the mid- or late-twentieth century, can easily become entangled. Tati is able to perceive

the everyday processes and procedures that one goes through, usually unconsciously. Tati's films speak to everyone because they concern themselves with the very systems of behavior and patterns of living of contemporary man. None of Tati's films seems dated. Both the subject matter and its treatment are as valid today as they ever were. With a general rising consciousness about over-industrialization and a stronger skepticism about what has been called progress, it is fascinating to observe how many of one's own observations on the social system begin to correspond with the insights Tati offered years ago. If Mon Oncle was taken to be merely a cute film in 1958, dealing with the insensitivity and lack of perception inherent on the daily lives of some people, today the same film seems to have taken on a more ominous and realistic tenor. The cold, glass skyscrapers of Playtime are amusing but they strike a common chord in everyone: "Are these structures really our idea of a place to live?" As the situations Tati has lampooned over the years become more life's norm, the laughter they generate becomes increasingly poignant.

Tati's films not only deal with common themes; they deal with them as entertainment, as farce, not as propaganda. The power of a revolutionary diatribe from Godard, or a preachy social message from Chaplin's later works, pales beside the lasting effect of watching Tati's characters deal with the world.

With the perspective offered only by time, one is able to view Tati's work from many levels. The social relevance of these films seems to increase as society nears crisis points in the environment, natural resources, transportation and a re-evaluation of basic human values. Tati's place within a new and concerned humanistic movement will be further examined.

This study attempts to place Tati's work in proper relationship to the early comedy film masters, as well as looking at the background of music hall and mime that originally led Tati to films. Each of Tati's films, including both a recent film made for Swedish television and his plans for a forthcoming feature, are analyzed as they relate to each other and to the overall body of Tati's work. Tati's growth as a film artist, able to use the medium, is explored through analysis of his use of camera, color, sound effects, music and setting. It is only through the observed relationships of Tati's films to society, to film heritage and to themselves that one can fully appreciate his contribution.   When the work of nearly thirty years of filmmaking is examined, one finds here much more than a string of light and oddly amusing comedies.   The waters run much deeper than one would expect at first glance.

CHAPTER 2

TATI AND HIS FILM HERITAGE

It is far easier to see Tati as a product of his film
heritage than to see him in any relation to his contemporaries. Tati's films are grounded in the French comedy film
tradition. One, of course, sees immediate parallels with
Chaplin and Keaton. But it must be remembered that Chaplin came, in part, out of the French tradition. Chaplin's admitted predecessor by a few short years was the French film
clown Max Linder. Linder himself was preceded by even earlier funny men of French cinema. If any one people had a
monopoly on screen comedy during the first years of the century, it was the French.

By the time Jacques Tati was born in Le Pecq, France,
in 1908, France was producing, among its vast film output of
the day, comedies and detective serials that were the standard
for the world. André Deed, a clown of the circus tradition,
had created a character named Gribouille, a simpleton in
white-face, a brother to Pierrot and Pagliaccio, according to
film historian Georges Sadoul. As early as 1906, Louis
Feuillade, who worked for the powerful Gaumont company,
starting producing comedies with trick effects in the manner of
his contemporary, Georges Méliès. "He understood how to
milk an absurd situation for all it was worth, drawing from it
a thousand lunatic consequences,"[6] according to Sadoul. The
comedy of the absurd was continued by a student of Feuillade,
Jean Durand, who directed two comedy series, the Onésime
and the Calinoconis. According to Sadoul, "Durand was a more
exacting artist than Feuillade or even Linder."[7]

If, as Walter Kerr says in his book The Silent Clowns,
Boireau, yet another film clown, would force his pursuers to
walk on the ceiling in order to catch him, and Tontolini, rolling down a flight of stairs, would wrap himself up in a carpet,

8

roll out the door and up the side of a nearby building, then the fantastical comedy devices that Tati makes his specialty have direct forerunners from decades earlier.

Max Linder developed a more sophisticated style of comedy. He did not employ the then common chase scenes, physical gags or trick effects. Linder, who entered films about the time of Tati's birth, created the first real screen character, the polished, sophisticated dandy who loses his dignity and then regains it. Tati's character, Hulot, who is by no means polished, carries himself with a great deal of dignity, which he is constantly losing, regaining and losing again. Hulot, however, is much less concerned for or aware of his own dignity than is Max.

After Linder's popularity had peaked, a number of refined film clowns and comedians began appearing on European screens, as a result of the influence of France's powerrul Pathé company. The U.S., lagging behind France, Italy, Russia and England, was about to concoct its own powerful blend of burlesque and vaudeville.

Charlie Chaplin quickly became the film clown. Over the course of a remarkably few years, starting with Mack Sennett in 1914, the English stage comedian brought to life a filmic persona that was to delight the entire world. Chaplin became the universal clown as his tramp character developed, revealing one facet of character after another, each, to some degree, common to all of us. The little tramp was indeed a comedy archetype. No one could improve on Chaplin's intuitive discovery. But there were other directions to explore, other archetypes to unearth. The persona we can associate only with Keaton was not to be fully realized for another five to six years. The first ten years of film comedy could now be seen to have been leading up to Chaplin.

It was only natural that the film-going public would compare Tati's characters (both François the postman, from Jour de Fête, and Monsieur Hulot) to Chaplin. Even the name "Hulot" sounds like Charlot, the name Chaplin was known by in France. Chaplin, who had extensive training in dance and pantomime, similar to Tati, emphasized his character's agility and grace. Charlie's fierce and lovable independence would get him into situations and his ballet-like agility would often get him out. Chaplin was ever aware of what he was doing in the physical universe. He enjoyed the "jungle gym" of the physical world and played around in it like a child.

Chaplin's comment on life seemed to be that it was a lot more
fun if one could stop battling with it and start dancing with it.
Many scenes from Chaplin's films which are intended to be
confrontations are actually skillfully and hilariously staged
dances. "If one simply rolls with the punches one won't get
hurt," seems to be what Charlie was constantly showing us.
And, if you can add a little dance step or a pirouette, it can
be all the more enjoyable.

Tati has constructed his films very similarly to Chaplin's early films, that is, as loose picaresque tales. Tati's
films are a string of incidents, each not necessarily connect-
ed to whatever precedes or follows it. Hulot goes from situation to situation and, though there may be a token storyline, is the only unifying element in the film. Just as Chaplin's world is one of pitfalls, traps and oversized adversaries,
Hulot's world is one of complex and nonsensical structures,
gadgets and social conventions, a world in which Hulot proceeds with great caution and some timidity. Hulot is unable
to escape the snares as effortlessly as Chaplin. Much of
Tati's humor involves Hulot walking headlong and heedlessly
into a situation he is ill-equipped to deal with. Chaplin's
awareness of the world around him is much greater than Hulot's; Hulot usually grasps the situation only after he is knee-
deep in it. Hulot, in all his dogged innocence, attempts to
extricate himself from his complicated and seemingly absurd
world. He attempts conscientiously to leave everything neatly
in its place, all the while upsetting most of what he comes in
contact with. Unlike Chaplin, Hulot is a man in the dark,
bumping into all the furniture.

As Hulot springs one trap after another and sends the
world crashing down around his ears, one gets an opportunity
to observe many of the things that permeate one's own life:
mindless architecture, silly appliances, endless traffic jams,
for example. Hulot's travails have a point: as he deals with
the world, one comes to observe things with a rare objectivity. In a sense, Hulot is a guinea pig for the sake of one's
improved perceptions. Chaplin's adventures, before Modern
Times, had no such ulterior motive. Charlie, himself, was
the reason for the film. Hulot, on the other hand, is not
the reason for Tati's films. As Armand J. Cauliez states
in his book on Tati: "The Chaplinesque personality is an end
in itself, the Tati-esque personage is more average. Hulot
is no more than a catalyst."[8]

If the character of Chaplin's tramp is the very reason
for the film, then it becomes necessary for him to inhabit
the frame almost constantly. Hulot, however, can come and
go. As the catalyst he need not remain to observe the chain
reactions he may have set off behind himself. Hulot is, in
fact, absent from the screen for entire comedy sequences in
both Playtime and Trafic. Given Tati's use of Hulot as a
catalyst or triggering element rather than the very subject,
film historian Basil Wright has stated that "as an artist he is
as individual as Chaplin, though narrower in range."[9] It is
not often necessary for Tati to draw upon his talents of mime,
dance, creation of gags and direction all at once. There is
much more happening in a Tati film than simply Hulot.

Hulot, like Chaplin, is perfectly suited to getting by
in a logical universe. Unlike Chaplin, he can not also function in an absurd universe. Hulot stumbles over and is
snared by the world's absurdities. He is nearly always in a
state of subdued panic. Chaplin's tramp seems to thrive on
most of what the world throws at him. The biggest exception to this is the Chaplin film which is most similar to a
Tati film: Modern Times. Here, for once, the world seems
a bit too much for little Charlie. He is figuratively and lit-
erally eaten alive by the wheels of monolithic technology. In
true Hulot fashion, Charlie is pushed from one absurd situation into another. Events take over and Charlie is not at all
in control. The theme of the film is remarkably close to
Tati's theme of the human spirit versus mindless technology.
For Chaplin, Modern Times was just one step in the growing
social consciousness of his films. Unlike Tati, though, Chaplin allowed his message to become dominant and his films began to take on the feel of propaganda. One of Tati's strengths
as a chronicler of the modern day is that he makes his views
so palatable. Tati's insights echo long after Chaplin's too obvious propaganda is forgotten.

Kerr states in The Silent Clowns that Chaplin's
strength rested in part on the fact that his comedy was always
to be played straight-faced; this same straight-faced quality
enables Tati's comedy to work, as well. Much like Max Linder, Hulot has no intention of appearing as anything less than
dignified. In his characteristically hazy state of awareness,
Hulot never realizes that he is funny. If Chaplin chooses to
play a hilarious scene with a straight face, it is because the
unexpected ease and nonchalance of the character will make the
scene all the funnier. This principle works for Tati, too,
though Hulot's deadpan dignity could never be interpreted as
nonchalance.

Chaplin has the preciosity of a child showing off.   He
is ever aware of his talents.   Hulot is never aware; never
aware that he does not fit into his surroundings, or that he
has egg on his face.   It is this lack of awareness, coupled
with Hulot's dignified expression, that makes his situation so
amusing.   Chaplin summed this up when he said: "If what
you're doing is funny, you don't need to be funny doing
it. "[10]

As Chaplin's popularity grew, so did his power in the
film industry.   He was able to spend more time on each of
his film projects and thereby allow his comedy impulses to
be more deeply realized.   Chaplin's opportunity to make his
films at his own pace came only after a number of years of
hectically produced one- and two-reelers.   Tati, on the other
hand, never assumed there was any way to make a film
other than the way one wanted.   Tati's sensibility, formed
over years as a solo stage performer, was never suited for
work as part of any studio system.   He has chosen, as Chaplin eventually did, to turn out only a few films, but these he
cares for passionately.   Tati's position as the overall creative force behind and arbiter of his films puts a great burden
onto his shoulders.   Just as Chaplin chose to do as much as
he could in his films, so has Tati chosen to write, act, direct and even decide the settings and the decor.   This does
not make for speedy film production or for efficiency.   It
does, however, allow for works of a highly personal vision.

Chaplin, who had initially resisted in the coming of
sound, began using elements of sound creatively in Modern
Times.   In that film, Chaplin, the master of the visual gag,
constructed comedy situations based solely upon the use of
sound.   The scene where Chaplin drinks tea with the minister's wife is funny because of the indelicate gurgling of
Charlie's stomach.   Similarly, Tati's films could not be considered silent films.   They are laced with minimal dialogue;
dialogue used as just another sound effect.   Tati emphasizes
the noise of the technological world and sets it off against
the sounds of nature.   The musical themes, in addition, are
chosen to correspond with the degree of chaos to which Hulot has reduced the world.

But Tati has maintained that while the comparisons
between himself and Chaplin are many, the differences are
even greater and, perhaps, more fundamental.   Tati sees a
more direct link between himself and Buster Keaton.   As

Cauliez has observed: "Between Chaplin and Tati there is an intermediate attitude; that of Buster Keaton."[11]

Many filmmakers have considered earlier filmmakers to be their spiritual fathers--Chaplin honored Linder as such, Eisenstein named Griffith. But fewer look the other way. Significantly, Buster Keaton considered Tati to be his spiritual son. Keaton had discovered another comedy archetype. His "Great Stoneface" showed only minimal emotion, very much to the same degree as the reserved Hulot. Keaton had a stage background of acrobatics and used solely his body for expressive purposes. Foreshadowing Hulot's wide-eyed objectivity pitted against a confusing and overbearing world, Keaton constantly represented himself as "the single unit against a dwarfing environment."[12] Keaton's world was not yet the over-industrialized wasteland of Tati's. Keaton placed himself in many settings with the theme of man versus the large machine. His extraordinary physical abilities allowed him to leap all over a speeding locomotive in The General or to climb about the rigging of a sailing ship in The Love Nest. Keaton was able to fuse himself with large, inanimate objects in order to avoid being overwhelmed by them. Much of Tati's comedy, however, is based upon Hulot's utter inability to fuse himself with any part of the world. Nevertheless, the confrontation of oversized machine and undersized man is basic to the comedy of both Keaton and Tati.

Like Chaplin, and unlike Tati, Keaton's storylines had a clear confrontation of characters and a clearly set goal for the main character to try to reach. Yet Keaton could easily get sidetracked from the goal (saving the girl, winning the girl) and spend his time devising elaborate contraptions and ingenious schemes to overcome any obstacles in his path. Hulot, however, rarely displays any fascination for the physical world. He does not know how things work, nor why. Hulot deals with the physical and technical world only so far as is necessary to get himself untangled from it.

Keaton's passion for gadgetry was far less important than his more fundamental experimentations with the very form of film. Keaton's gadgetry was a sidelight to achieving his own filmmaking goal; Tati's passion for observing machinery and gadgetry is a goal in itself. Tati's farcical analysis of everyday machinery is made all the funnier by his character, Hulot's, timidity. Long stretches of Tati's films revolve around ingenious machines. In Tati's latest completed feature, Trafic, Hulot is assigned to transport a multi-

faceted camping vehicle from Paris to an Amsterdam auto
show. A number of the scenes in the film are devoted to
demonstrating the vehicle's startling array of unexpected devices: seats that fold down to form a bed, a car horn that
detaches for use as an electric shaver, a detachable engine
grill that swings forward to form an outdoor barbecue. Many
of Tati's scenes are based upon the transformation or break-
down of a machine or industrial object. A runaway spare
tire, covered with wet leaves, becomes a funeral wreath in
Les Vacances de Monsieur Hulot. In the same film Hulot
goes paddling in a kayak. When the boat breaks in half
across the middle and slams shut upon Hulot like a book, it
takes the shape of the mouth of a large fish sticking out of
the water.

The entire climactic sequence from Playtime is the
gradual and well calculated disintegration of a newly built
nightclub. As objects begin to function incorrectly and to
fall apart, there is revealed a clear thought process behind
each object's disintegration. Ceiling decorations, strung from
wires, slip down too far and form a fence, complete with
gate, behind which a group of raucous customers stage their
own "private" party. The glass front door shatters, leaving
the doorman holding onto the metal handle. He continues to
swing his arm back and forth, allowing people to pass in and
out through the imaginary door. This methodical destruction
of objects is, obviously, amusing, but it serves another of
Tati's purposes as well. There is a certain rare insight one
can acquire only when something is picked apart; only when
an action or an object is looked at piecemeal. What is the
purpose of a front door if no one notices that it is missing?
What is the point of fancy decorations if they offer people
more enjoyment by falling apart? How meaningful is a funeral wreath, or the funeral itself, if a leaf-covered tire is
placed reverently by the graveside? It is common for Hulot
to find himself in an over-gadgeted, over-designed setting
such as the Arpel's ultra-modern household in Mon Oncle, the
auto show in Trafic or the entire studio-built Paris of Playtime. Tati, unencumbered by plot devices and character development, finds these explorations of this "best of all possible worlds" to be quite enough to base a film upon.

The character Keaton played possessed great patience.
He was ever able to accept and then contend with the roadblocks life threw up in his path; his patience was a result of
his adaptability. Hulot also possesses a great deal of patience. He is able to let each incident roll off him as he

moves on to the next, his desire to participate unabated. In
Les Vacances Hulot goes from one disastrous summer resort
activity to the next without breaking stride. The fact that he
may have just driven everyone off the tennis court with his
eccentric and powerful serve does not mean that he will not
be ready that evening in full pirate costume, for a masquerade dance. The fact that no one else comes to the party
does not stop Hulot from dancing with the girl. Although the
results may be greatly different, Hulot's quiet enthusiasm is
similar to Keaton's dogged persistence. Each character's patience is the element necessary to keep him in the struggle
with life.

        Keaton, Chaplin and Tati all had a simple, straight-
forward approach to the use of the camera. All three men
valued the long shot for its ability to reveal the entire body.
Just as Chaplin wanted none of his movements robbed of
their full effect by having his legs cut off below the frame,
Tati's years of stage experience also developed his entire
body as an expressive element. His deemphasis of expression for Hulot's face, together with his accentuation of the
body, accounts in part for his dislike of the close-up. Keaton used wide-angle shots not simply to emphasize his body
movements, but to maintain the believability of his stunts.
He feared that any change of a camera angle in the middle of
a stunt would cause his elaborate gags to seem staged or to
appear as though a stuntman were actually doing them. In
addition, Keaton used the wide-angle camera set-up to
heighten the disparity in size between man and machine. This
simple technique is employed by Tati to dwarf Hulot in the
cityscape of Playtime.

        In Steamboat Bill Jr. Keaton is seen standing at the
bottom of the frame, a tiny figure. Behind him stands the
massive facade of a building. The building crashes forward,
falling down upon the unperturbed Keaton in such a manner
that an open window falls exactly where Keaton stands. He
is untouched. This is a good example of Keaton's emphasis
of relative sizes. One of the earliest shots in Tati's Trafic
is a high-angled long shot that looks down upon the vast
floor of the auto exposition hall. A group of men scurry
about, stretching long strings to designate the location for
each car's display. The characters are dwarfed by the immensity of the hall. The humor in this spacious set-up
comes from watching as each of the officials high steps his
way over each string and moves about the hall. From the
distant camera angle one no longer sees the strings that were

visible in an earlier, much closer shot. The group of self-important officials appears to be doing a ridiculous birdlike strut. It is interesting to note that one of the distant officials is played by Tati himself. His lanky movements stand out even at that great a distance. The visual gag works here because of the distance and immensity of the shot. Much of Playtime conveys this same feeling of humanity dwarfed by its surroundings. Tati's reluctance to push his camera in for tight and intimate closeups has allowed him to discover many benefits in using the long shot and in keeping the audience's point of view at a distance.

One of the factors that adds so much to the special quality of the gags staged by Tati and his predecessors, Chaplin, Keaton and Lloyd, is that none of the gags involve total fantasy. They all have a base in reality. The audience is aware that if certain conditions existed the very thing that just happened to Hulot could, indeed, happen to them. Gags can be more delightful when one senses that they are staged wholly within the restrictions of physical laws. Very little of the comedy of Tati or any of his predecessors is like an animated cartoon, most of which operate at some point outside of those laws. If it can be said that Keaton, Chaplin and Lloyd, as acrobats, exploited the physical extremes of the human body, then Tati exploits coincidence and timing. In The Boat Keaton stands erect in his sinking vessel and unflinchingly allows the water to rise until he is totally submerged. Only his hat remains floating on top of the water. Had one the physical discipline of Keaton one would be able to perform the same stunt. In Les Vacances Tati attempts to paint a beached kayak. By directorially using no methods more supernatural than plain, everyday coincidence he creates a hilarious scene. The paint can which rests in the sand beside the boat is picked up by an incoming wave and is washed in and out precisely in time to meet Hulot's brush each time it is lowered. It is all precise and delightful timing.

Occasionally, it is true, Tati does cross the boundary of the physically possible, as did the early greats. As Hulot cranks up his auto to fix a flat tire in Les Vacances we watch as one of the women sitting in the back seat starts to rise with each turn of the crank. In Playtime a plastic model airplane droops its wings as the heat in the new nightclub rises and raises its wings back up as the temperature is lowered. It must, however, be noted that Tati and his mentors take physical reality as a challenge to be met, not as something to be discarded. It seems natural that Chaplin, Keaton and Tati, with strong backgrounds in the absolute reality of stage performance, would deal imaginatively with the world according to its own physical limits.

It is interesting to note that Keaton's films are filled with chases and perilous stunts. He continually pushes himself to the brink of his physical capabilities. Tati, on the other hand, constructs his films with incidents so commonplace as to seem ridiculous. Hulot very rarely attempts to do more than simply walk from one place to another. Playtime is built upon Hulot's looking for a man with whom he has a business appointment. The plot of Trafic is constructed upon Hulot's getting a car from Paris to Amsterdam. In one Keaton film, Cops, Buster takes on the uncharacteristically simple task of transporting a wagonload of furniture across town. In the fashion of Tati the simple chore complicates itself to the point where Keaton is being chased by the entire police force. Keaton's lack of awareness that he is riding his wagon straight through the center of a policeman's parade is similar to Hulot's more general obliviousness. In The General, Keaton is busy chopping wood to stoke the furnace of his speeding locomotive. He does not even notice that he is speeding through the heart of the enemy force. If Keaton's awareness can occasionally dip as low as Hulot's, as shown here, his resolve and ingenuity in dealing with any ensuing situation are far superior to Hulot's. Unlike Keaton, Hulot will become frightened and intimidated. Although he possesses great energy, Hulot is less the man of action than the man of intimidation when faced with any sort of opposition. As Hulot chases his runaway car tire in Les Vacances he runs right into the center of a funeral in progress. Hulot, rather than offend anyone and because he simply can think of no way out, stands patiently in the reception line and greets everyone as if he were part of the proceedings.

Keaton's deadpan face was always a funny incongruity. The situation he might be in could be terrifying and yet his face betrayed nothing. If there were great emotions raging beneath the surface they were rarely revealed. Hulot's deadpan is, curiously enough, not a contrast between emotion and expression; his emotions are uncannily low key. Tati, like Keaton, juxtaposes the catastrophic situation with the calm reaction. Hulot's detachment from the world is such that he absorbs little; his face reveals all he knows. Keaton absorbs much, with a certain shrewdness. It seems his mind races so quickly that his face has little time to form an expression.

In Walter Kerr's The Silent Clowns, this sensitive analysis of Keaton's character seems to come amazingly close to that of Hulot's:

> Keaton's growth would not be a matter of finding a character for the film in which he was to be seen. The film as independent, self-defining object became his goal; though he was everlastingly present in the film, he was present as possessed rather than possessing. As a performer, as a personality, he was sharply defined, more rigidly so than most.... But how little he asks of us, as a person! He asks for no emotional response whatever; no fears, no tears, no satisfaction in triumph. No intimacy; he will not confide in us, not tell us what he is thinking, not even smile.[13]

Although Keaton is remarkably graceful, it seems that his gags come mainly from his speed and physical strength. Tati, on the other hand, possesses simple gracefulness. Keaton may be seen at his best scurrying straight up the side of a wall; Hulot is at his best winding his long-limbed way around the water fountains, channels and garden bric-à-brac strewn about the Arpels' front yard in Mon Oncle.

Keaton's concerns were with the form of film much more than with the development of film characters. Keaton realized the extent to which film had "falsified reality; Keaton would be that false and no more."[14] He capitalized on the peculiarities of film as opposed to reality, turning what most considered disadvantages into advantages. Keaton was a film artist in the truest sense of the term; he used the qualities of the medium to do what film alone could do. To Keaton, film had its own integrity. It was not simply a tool for recording someone else's art form. Tati's approach to the medium, however, is more stagebound. It is Tati who feels that one of the advantages of the wide-angle shot is that it most closely approximates the stage. Like the stage, it allows the audience to select which character or piece of action it will watch. A keener outlook on reality is usually Tati's underlying goal. Whereas Keaton, unconcerned with reality, concerns himself with film form. The way film handles reality; the very qualities of the medium are the things that fascinate Keaton. Film is, for Tati, much more of a recording process than it ever was for Keaton.

Harry Langdon, who is considered to be the fourth great silent film clown, is rarely ranked with Chaplin, Keaton and Lloyd. Langdon was a less substantial filmmaker, filling in the spaces left by the other masters. Langdon's childish, innocent film character was as out of place as Hulot in any social situation. Both film characters are ill-at-ease with the simplest of human contacts. It is as if both were raised by a species of moon men. Langdon, whose innocence can, at times, make even Hulot appear world weary, is placed in perspective to Hulot by Philip Strick:

> The tragedy of Hulot's comedy is thus basically standard; his embarrassment with the problem of what to do with himself when dealing with other people is connected with his height but is also the result of inner remoteness, identical with that suffered by Langdon and Keaton....[15]

Langdon's slow pace of thought has been described by Walter Kerr: "His thoughts come one at a time, with intermissions."[16] Langdon's slowly paced approach to life is all the funnier in comparison to the car chases, fist fights and general confusion he often wanders into. Hulot's slowness of thought is similar to Langdon's. Hulot seems only to be concerned with the present; the disaster of a moment ago is forgotten. Both Hulot and Langdon have the ability to involve themselves totally in what they are doing. They both possess great passion for participating in life. Harry, like a child imitating his elders, waits to catch certain cues from the people around him and acts accordingly. Langdon's need to be accepted by the people around him is only a bit less disguised than Hulot's. It becomes quite funny when innocent looking little Harry occasionally reveals his amorous intentions toward women or when he breaks into a hearty laugh, imitating his companions, only to far exceed everyone else's enthusiasm. Hulot will bare his true soul as well. In Les Vacances he approaches his very brief tennis game with an excess of gusto. In Mon Oncle he will want desperately to mingle with the guests at the Arpel's chic cocktail party. Going overboard, Hulot ends up recounting an off-color story to everyone's embarrassment. Hulot and Langdon are both characters who wait on the sidelines hoping to be called upon. In their desire to relate to others, coupled with their own inexperience, they usually respond inappropriately or with too much energy. They both seem destined to remain inside themselves.

One of the most endearing qualities of both Hulot and Langdon is that neither character is able to hold resentment. There are no feuds or underlying animosities in either of their films. Neither character, it seems, notices when and if he has been treated badly. Langdon has the innocence of a child and is able to forgive his "elders" as quickly and as totally as any child can.

Both Hulot and Langdon are easily intimidated. Hulot definitely registers guilt and fear each time he sees the hotel keeper in Les Vacances staring menacingly at him. Hulot realizes when he has done something wrong and is quick to cover it up or to run from it. As the disgruntled hotel keeper stares at muddy footprints leading across his lobby to the coat rack, one realizes that Hulot is hiding among the coats, shuddering like a frightened child.

Just as Harry will imitate the behavior of those around him in order to fit in, so will Hulot unthinkingly and automatically enter into any activity in order to be accepted. One of the simplest examples of this, again in Les Vacances, is when Hulot seizes the opportunity to carry a backpack up a nearby hillside for a young lady he does not even know. He spots her in the lobby of the little hotel and automatically lends her a hand. No introductions or explanations are necessary. Hulot is not even concerned with meeting the girl; he simply wants to participate with other people.

Behind the more or less obvious connections between Langdon and Tati is one that can easily go unnoticed. Langdon was a direct outgrowth from and reaction to the comedy of his day. His character was formulated upon a groundwork of comedy characters and conventions that had already been set down by earlier comedians. Langdon could not have been understood nor could he have existed as one of the very first screen clowns. His character needed an established framework inside of which to grow. Walter Kerr described him as "punctuation" in the "sentence" that was silent comedy. Tati, in the same sense, is an outgrowth of his own day. He produces films with very contemporary themes. Yet, Tati often takes an old-fashioned technical and story approach. Hulot's speechlessness is much funnier than if he were a character in an actual silent film. The fact that Hulot can speak (one does get to hear him now and then) but hardly ever does, makes him all the more amusing. The fact that the conversations of Tati's characters are reduced to nothing more than vocal sound effects is not just funny but gives one an insight into the value of most people's (and most film's) dialogue. Tati's lack of dramatic story structure is also effective in comparison to the taut dramatic structuring of films today. Tati's films do not fall into any contemporary categories, but fall rather into the spaces between those categories.

In describing the position of Langdon's screen character, Walter Kerr might just as well be describing Tati's Hulot:

> The fact that we can not define him, pigeon-hole him, teach him to see reason, becomes his tantalizing hold on us. He is, at his best, an enchanting unknowable, following his own inhibited toe-dance without apology for its peculiarities. [17]

To put the last of the great silent clowns, Harold Lloyd, into a context with Tati proves more difficult. Lloyd's character, the bright-eyed, optimistic, All-American boy, was developed only after years of experimentation. The "glasses character," as he was soon called due to his pair of dark, round rimmed glasses, came into being only after Lloyd had dropped the artifices of his earlier characters. Unlike Chaplin, Keaton, or Langdon, or Tati as well, Lloyd's new screen personality was remarkably close to Lloyd's own personality. His character seemed to be a model young man, the type all America admired: hard working, energetic, enterprising and eternally optimistic. Where Keaton and later Tati might seem odd to an audience and at the same time might shed some light into the darker corners of their minds, Lloyd simply reinforced his contemporary audience's concepts of behavior.

Lloyd was, first and foremost, a physical clown. He did not deal with the character subtleties or sentimentality of Chaplin. His abilities were closer to Keaton's daredevil acrobatics. Lloyd made breathtaking physical stunts his specialty. Unlike Keaton, Lloyd's reaction to the situation he was in was always that of a common person. Hanging off the face of a fifteen-story building or crawling from girder to girder atop a skyscraper under construction, Lloyd's reaction was always the same: he was terrified. Lloyd designed his films simply for the purpose of thrills and laughter; certainly reason enough for their existence. Tati has constructed his films to work on the level of Lloyd's as well as on the level of farce. If Lloyd, in Hot Water, takes the

family for a near disastrous automobile ride it is not his
purpose for the audience to stop and take a look at the convention of the automobile anew.   Tati, in Trafic for example,
wants the audience to see the automobile from a fresh point
of view.

Tati and Lloyd do, however, parallel each other in
certain aspects of their work.   Tati and Lloyd come closest
in their characterizations of men who become innocently and
unwillingly entangled in overwhelming situations.   In Lloyd's
Feet First he has stowed away aboard ship in a mail sack.
The sack eventually gets delivered with Harold still inside
and, through Harold's squirming about, manages to land on
a scaffold being raised up the front of a tall building.   What
follows is one of Lloyd's most thrilling sequences as he attempts, desperately, to climb to safety.   Lloyd's character,
a man of normal perceptions, must be engulfed by situations
only through the most elaborate of plot devices, as shown
above.   Tati's Hulot, a man of quite odd and selective perceptions, can fall into a comedy situation very simply.   Hulot walks into predicaments with the innocence of a child:
the kayak that collapses in Les Vacances or the ivy cover-
ing of a house pulled down in Trafic.   Lloyd's unmasked
enthusiasm and Hulot's quiet desire to participate are in
many ways the same.   Both characters usually wind up over
their heads.

A scene from Lloyd's The Freshman shows Harold at
a college party wearing a rented, although not quite sewn
together, tuxedo.   As Harold tries to keep up appearances,
a drunken tailor sneaks about, concealed behind curtains and
furniture, vainly trying to sew together the disintegrating
suit.   The gags and overall situation are similar to Tati.
Hulot, trying desperately to fit into the Arpel's cocktail
party; not wanting to reveal his uneasiness or fright, is
similar to Harold at the party trying to keep his "act"
together.   Here one sees Harold as more than a man
caught in a dangerous situation. He is a man who tries
to win the acceptance of the people around him. A
sense of human need and of sympathy is set up here. Hulot in his pirate costume, the only man to show up for
the masquerade dance in Les Vacances, creates the same
reaction.   The sense Hulot creates of a lonely man, a
man one would like to protect is an uncommon feeling in
a Lloyd film and all the more precious when it does oc-
cur.

One fundamental difference between Tati and the early silent clowns is that Hulot is an older man and the characters created by Chaplin, Keaton, Lloyd and Langdon are all young men. Lloyd made a virtue of his youth and exuberance, Langdon was practically a child, and Keaton and Chaplin built many of their situations upon boy meets girl. Hulot is a gentleman who moves at the distracted pace of an older person, whose perceptions are similarly slowed down and whose distance from amorous encounters is the same distance properly prescribed for a gentleman of some years. What is interesting is that the Hulot character was fully formed as early as Les Vacances, a film made when Tati was in his early forties. Tati, most likely, did not create Hulot as an elderly type. It was, however, Hulot's natural diffidence and underplayed quality that allowed the character to slip so naturally into old age. Hulot's romantic encounters are, accordingly, flimsy in nature and not the motivating factors in the plot.

The lack of dialogue in Tati's films initiate many of the comparisons made with silent comedies. While the substantial comparisons go far beyond that of sound or silence it must be noted that the best silent comedies used the fewest title cards. Tati's films, which never rely on the spoken word, require few, if any, subtitles when shown in other countries. Silent films with full musical scores could hardly be considered silent; Tati's work relies upon full orchestration. Tati, however, does not arbitrarily limit himself to simply the technical possibilities available to silent films. The intricate and expressive sound effects that Tati builds into his soundtracks are crucial to his comedy and are things the early silent clowns could only have dreamed of. One might ask why Tati takes advantage of only some of the many technical aspects of modern filmmaking and ignores the potential for humorous dialogue. Walter Kerr, in describing the benefits of silence, seems to answer this question:

> The fantasy born of silence was simply one more gift dropped in the laps of men determined to outwit reality. A portion of that unpleasant universe had already been destroyed, thank you. How much easier to get around! Their imaginations were released along with their limbs, and no voice could be heard to say them nay. I don't know--I don't believe that anyone ever cared whether comedy found a voice. [18]

Another characteristic of silent comedies is the speed at which the film moved. The fast paced movements of the silent clowns is perhaps their most well-known characteristic. The great silent clowns were able to turn this "undercranked" look into an advantage. According to Walter Kerr, it was this rapid speed that enabled men like Chaplin, Keaton and Lloyd to create characters even more extraordinary than they would be at a natural speed. Kerr maintains that had silent comedies been filmed and projected at the natural speeds of today's films one would perceive the great silent clowns differently. They would no longer be the superhuman characters one imagines them to be but, rather, normally encumbered although quite talented human beings. The little extra speed gave the silent clowns the edge needed to seem free of gravity's pull and the body's limitations. One of the differences between Hulot and his predecessors is the speed with which he moves through the world. It is not simply a function of old cameras versus new, it is also a function of Hulot's very personality. Hulot never moves more quickly than absolutely necessary. Tati suits his character to the slower pace of modern sound films just as the earlier clowns suited their characters to the then current nature of the medium. Hulot appears as an average human being, albeit eccentric in his pitched-forward, gangly walk. When he does find it necessary to break into a sudden flurry of movement and activity it seems all the funnier by comparison to his normal subdued state.

Tati is a filmmaker who is aware of his heritage. He will often make references to Chaplin and Keaton in interviews and lectures. After Mon Oncle had won the Academy Award in 1959 for Best Foreign Film, Tati made it a point to visit Mack Sennett. Tati arranged a party at Sennet's retirement home, using the opportunity to invite three other favorites: Stan Laurel, Harold Lloyd and Buster Keaton.

CHAPTER 3

TATI'S EARLY YEARS

Both Tati's father and maternal grandfather were
picture framers. It was assumed that Jacques would follow
in their footsteps and continue the prosperous business. At
the age of sixteen, Jacques was sent to a college of arts
and engineering to prepare for his future career. Tati was
able to find his way to England as a young man and while
employed there developed a passion for the game of rugby.
Penelope Gilliat, referring to these early days as an ama-
teur athelete, said:

> It would have been fine to see him on the field,
> six foot four of him, apparently always with a way
> of being able to lean alertly in any direction, as
> though he were balanced against a gale. The tilt
> is generally forward, exposing an eager five or
> six inches of striped sock. ... [19]

It was during these early years in England that Tati started
entertaining his friends with spontaneous pantomimes satirizing their own rugby matches. It must have been at this
time that he started developing the famous Hulot posture described by Gilliat above. As the enthusiasm of his friends
increased, Tati created more pantomimes until he had an
entire series of sports pantomimes to present whenever the
opportunity arose. These early creations would last throughout Tati's career, appearing in many forms in his films,
the tennis sequence from Les Vacances being the best-known
and most obvious.

Tati's eventual decision to become a pantomimist and
impressionist also had its roots in his early childhood. Tati has described himself as having been a visually oriented
child. His most vivid memories have to do with visually
comic scenes:

25

Even today I would shoot my first communion. I
can see my grandmother whom I loved very much.
This is perhaps why I start out to do a little slapstick comedy--it grew out of a strong visual mem-
ory. Comedy grows out of observation of people.[20]

In the same style as Max Linder, Tati started working in cafés doing one-night stands. His repertory consisted
of his rugby sketch, with him playing the goalie, players and
the crowd, and some newer sketches with titles such as
"The Tram Journey" and "The Fishing Party." Tati spent
a number of penniless years, unable to get work, until finding himself, one day, on the bill with Maurice Chevalier at
the Ritz. Despite nervousness and an unusual reluctance to
go on stage, which caused him to appear last, Tati was a
hit. Tati subsequently toured Europe performing in music
halls and circuses. He would have made it to the U.S. had
war not broken out in 1939.

The popular French author Colette was a supporter
of Tati's work. She drew attention to it vigorously. In
1936 she wrote in Le Journal:

Henceforth, I believe no festive, artistic or acrobatic spectacle could equal the displays given by
this astonishing man who has invented something
which includes dancing, sport, satire and pageant-
ry. He has created at the same time the player,
the ball and the racket; the balloon and the person
floating in it; the boxer and his adversary; the
bicycle and the cyclist. His powers of suggestion
are those of a great artist.[21]

Tati's pantomimes seemed to be based on lessening
the importance of the face and increasing the importance of
the body. Tati has repeatedly referred to a clown's need
for expressive legs. He points out yet another similarity
between himself and Keaton when he mentions Keaton's use
of the legs. Tati has said: "On the legs, for me, Keaton
is number one. You could have done a soundtrack, a dialogue, on his legs; interrogation, then decision, finally
fear."[22]

Tati is aware of another connection between his film
work and his years on the stage. The fickle nature of live
audiences has taught him the importance of shaving down his

performance to just the bare essentials, to what works and
nothing more. Tati has said: "It's impossible to do a comic
film without first having learned your craft on the stage,
through contact with the public. Otherwise, one is doing
literary comedy."[23] It is important in analyzing Tati's
films, never to lose sight of the man as a stage performer.
Tati has not left the stage behind for films; periodically he
returns. In 1961 he effectively transferred many of the gags
from his first feature film, Jour de Fête, to a stage production: "Jour de Fête à Olympia," which was a big success.

Tati's sense of observation made him aware of the
humor in everyday people. He wanted to present this realistic comedy in a "democratic" way, one that would not
spotlight him alone, as did his stage performances. Tati
found film to be the natural expression of his ideas.

The state of the Depression-era French film industry
was, according to film historian Georges Sadoul, uninspired.
He said that "the quantitative increase in film production only meant greater opportunities for second-rate work."[24]
René Clair and Jean Renoir were producing some of the best
work of the period and certainly showed expertise at handling
comedy. Clair, who displays a love of older films, both in
content and style, had a great respect for comedy pioneers
like Max Linder and Feuillade. In his Le Silence Est d'Or,
made in 1946, well after the Depression, he pays tribute to
the early silent cinema. Clair's orientation to older film
styles was very similar to Tati's soon to be expressed
style. Roy Armes wrote of Clair:

> Like another of the masters who influenced him
> profoundly, Charlie Chaplin, Clair remains a con-
> servative in his approach to the medium. He con-
> ceives of film as something to be acted out in
> front of a camera rather than a spectacle created
> directly with the camera.[25]

Clair did not characteristically concern himself with
social problems. His A Nous la Liberté does deal with the
soullessness of modern life but finds it necessary to close
in a utopia of leisure. Clair's love for light comedy and a
certain Capra-esque sentimentality seemed to water down the
social significance of his films. Tati, however, was able to
bridge the gap between light comedy and a substantial social
message by presenting his themes as bold satire. Clair's
Le Dernier Milliardaire is indeed a spoof on the existing so-

cial structure but, as Georges Sadoul has pointed out, it lacked a necessary audacity. Tati, on the other hand, is able to drive his points home through that very audacity.

It must be pointed out that Tati's use of minimal dialogue was not as revolutionary as one would think. Clair, at the height of the sound film's first popularity, felt that sound and dialogue used for its own sake was absurd. Arthur Knight has written:

> In Sous les Toits de Paris (1929), Le Million (1931) and A Nous la Liberté (1931), he worked with a minimum of dialogue, using music, choruses and sound effects to counterpoint and comment upon his visuals. In this principle of asynchronous sound ... Clair discovered a new freedom and fluidity for the sound medium. [26]

Jean Renoir, in early sound films like Boudu Sauvé des Eaux and Le Crime de Monsieur Lange, created some of the finest French comedies of the Depression decade. Boudu Sauvé des Eaux presented the tale of Boudu, a thoroughly anti-social, or more accurately a-social, tramp who is saved from drowning and befriended by a clerk, a typically bourgeois family man. Boudu, beautifully played in all his near-savagery by Michel Simon, is taken into the clerk's home. What follows is a hilarious and revealing clash between lifestyles. Although Boudu is aggressive and never allows any situation to get the better of him, he presents the same innocent, uncalculated and objective point of view on the social order as does Hulot some two decades later. Cauliez, in his book Jacques Tati, compares the two characters as he raises some doubt about both Hulot's and Boudu's actual freedom from society:

> Hulot himself like Renoir's Boudu ... resists the chains (conjugal, professional, etc.). But he depends on them more tightly than others. Boudu begs his bread and Hulot bows to the decisions of his brother-in-law. [27]

Tati's earliest experiment with film was in 1931. He filmed one of his stage routines, Oscar, Champion de Tennis. The film, never actually completed, serves as little more than Tati's introduction to the techniques of getting a performance onto film. The tennis pantomime was, of course, repeated, in part, years later in Les Vacances.

Tati's next venture was entitled On Demande une Brute. Made in 1934, this was Tati's first complete film. Tati enlisted the help of Charles Barrois as director and the young René Clément as assistant director. The script, which Tati collaborated on with Alfred Sauvy, was characteristically simple. It concerned a meek and mild man who is dominated by his shrewish wife. The man accidentally gets the reputation of being a champion wrestler and the obvious complications arise when he is forced to take on a real wrestler in the ring. Strong comparisons can be made here between this film and the early Sennett boxing comedy, The Knockout, starring Arbuckle with Chaplin in an early role playing the referee. Chaplin's brilliantly choreographed boxing sequence from City Lights comes to mind as well. There is also an early Lloyd short using the boxing motif: Harold, the inexperienced boxer, is led to the ring as he continues to read a book entitled "How to Box." Tati's choice of subject is, then, not unique but as Claude Beylie has observed, something far more important happened in the creation of this film. Tati started to formulate the comedy archetype that was eventually to be named Hulot. Beylie has written:

> The film marks the birth of an absolutely new comic character; clumsy, ungainly, reminiscent of a rope dancer, not knowing what to do with his immense size.... The basis of Tati's comedy is not farce or clowning but this sort of semi-vegetative unconsciousness which renders him totally unresponsible for what happens to him. [28]

The following year, 1935, saw Tati's next short film: Gai Dimanche. This time Tati allowed Jacques Berr to direct and cast the clown Rhum opposite himself. Philip Strick described Tati's film character as a "luckless dandy"[29] who does not quite hide his penniless state behind his one good suit of clothes. Tati appears at the beginning of the film out of the mouth of a Métro stop where he has spent the night. A street hawker who is also a friend gets Tati to accompany him on a picnic in the country. After an elaborate series of mechanical difficulties with the car (shades of Trafic) and after a variety of gastronomic problems the picnic ends in chaos. Both Beylie and Strick agree that the film is generally uninspired and clumsy in sections, offering Tati only few outlets for his talents. But, as Strick affirmed, progress was unmistakable. Placing this film in context with Tati's later films, Strick pointed out that

> The central character, endeavoring to fit himself
> into surroundings that are unwilling to accept his
> gangling frame, has an obvious affinity with Hu-
> lot.[30]

He further observed that the film's soundtrack foreshadowed
Tati's later works by its simple mixture of natural, outdoor
sounds with mechanical sounds.

Beylie as well sees firm connections between this
crude story of the hapless band of picnickers and the films
that were to follow twenty and thirty years later. Citing
early use of sound gags Beylie described a number of
scenes:

> A baby hidden inside the car where he imitates the
> sound of the motor.... A little girl stands on the
> top of a hill and blows into a trumpet (which on
> the sound track sounds like a hunting horn) while
> the group of adults run around her chasing a
> chicken they wish to have for lunch....[31]

Probably the greatest contribution this film made was
as yet another step closer to the completion of Tati's full
filmic character. In Beylie's words:

> Nevertheless the character one sees is already
> starting to stand out timidly, the future character
> tossed about by events, moved lazily by the wind,
> similar to a signal flag that is in a unique sense
> becoming a weather vane.[32]

Soigne Ton Gauche was Tati's next film. Made in
1936 it was directed by René Clément, written by Tati. According to Beylie, this film marks the first full flowering of
Tati's talent on film: "The genius of Tati this time totally
bursts forth as a result of the freedom Tati has and as a result of staging done a bit more intelligently than in the earlier films."[33] The film is full of the symbols and leitmotifs
that Tati has so far used throughout his film career. The
locations are an early example of the rustic, real-life locations Tati was to use a decade later in Jour de Fête. The
striped sweater Tati wears is definitely a precursor to Hulot's eccentrically striped socks. There is a blundering postman (Tati's main character in Jour de Fête will be just such
a blundering postman). There is even a gang of kids (a gang
of kids plays an important thematic role in Mon Oncle). The

farm boy boxing an invisible opponent in the barn is a perfect representation of "the combative nature of Tati".[34]
The overall feel of the film is one of watching real people
in real locations. There is that semi-documentary sense to
the proceedings that will not admit any false gloss. Beylie
sees in this short film a sharp focus on the elements that
make Tati's film characters different from Chaplin or Keaton or Langdon. Tati emerges from the film as the eternal
and optimistic competitor "who dreams of conquering the
world."[35] It does not matter how often or how suddenly he
is beaten. The quiet but relentless competitive spirit is the
very core of Tati's first feature, Jour de Fête, about a
speedcrazed bicycling mailman who is out to deliver the mail
faster than ever before. Les Vacances de Monsieur Hulot
appears at times to be no more than a string of gags cen-
tering around Hulot's spirit to compete and win at horseback
riding, tennis and ping-pong--in this film one senses that
Hulot wants to "out vacation" everyone at the hotel and
would not know how to relax even if he wanted to.

     After Soigne Ton Gauche Tati produced his next short
film entirely on his own. Retour à la Terre, made in 1938,
was a minor film compared with the earlier works. This
film suffered from the same poor editing that had marred
the earlier films but also continued to deal with Tati's rustic backgrounds and basic subjects. As in the earlier films,
Tati plays his character with the broad mannerisms he had
learned in the music hall.

     World War II interrupted Tati's career for six years.
While in the army Tati was stationed for a time in the country village of Ste.-Sévère-sur-Indre which gave him not only
the inspiration for Jour de Fête but the actual setting as well.
It was also, while in the army, that Tati met the man upon
whom Hulot would be most closely based.

CHAPTER 4

TATI'S FIRST FEATURE

After the war Tati played minor roles in two feature films directed by his friend Claude Autant-Lara. Sylvie et le Fantôme, made in 1945, has Tati seen only in double exposure, playing a gentle ghost in an old chateau. Tati spends the course of the film doing hardly anything more than walking around the secret passageways of the old house. The performance is disappointing because Tati gets no opportunity for physical comedy. Autant-Lara's next film, Le Diable au Corps, made the following year, shows Tati briefly as one of a group of soldiers seen huddled around a piano, celebrating the 1918 Armistice.

Tati returned to making his own films with a short entitled L'Ecole des Facteurs (School for Postmen). Tati returned to the country village of Ste.-Sévère-sur-Indre where he had spent time during the war. Here he created the character of François, the long-legged, bicycling postman out to deliver the mail in record time. Interestingly enough, Tati considers all his short films except this one to be of poor quality. This is the film Tati will come to mention most often as the beginning of his film career. On this project he worked with Henri Marquet, later to be a consultant to Tati on both Jour de Fête and Les Vacances. The short film cost Tati a few thousand dollars and was so successful that Tati decided to make the idea into a feature-length film.

Finding some $30,000 more from two different backers, Tati was able to make his first feature. Jour de Fête (Day of the Festival) was constructed around Tati's portrayal of François the postman, introduced to the public in the previous short film. The mood of the film is well conveyed by the review in The New York Times:

> The story of François, a postman of St. Sevère.
> He is happy in his work, casually delivering the
> mail, while cycling through the countryside with
> professional éclat. He is not averse to stopping
> for a chat or helping with the haying. That is
> until the carnival makes its annual visit.[36]

The carnival or fête is a simple traveling show which passes through town once a year, spending one day, and one day
only, in the village. Naturally the villagers look upon the
event with great excitement. François, the hero, is much
impressed by a newsreel shown in the traveling cinema.
The subject of the film is the high efficiency of the American postal system. The villagers begin to kid François a-
bout his slow-paced mail service. He energetically takes
up what he assumes to be a new challenge: deliver the mail
à la América. The Times review notes that "François filled with inspiration and local wine, speeds around the area
with the abandon of a drunken sailor...."[37]

     The film is very simply structured, with one slap-
stick gag linked to the next. Behind the film's simplicity
are the conflicts that Tati will carry through his films to
come: man versus machine, the Old World versus the new
and efficiency versus inefficiency. The film begins with the
arrival of the carousel's wooden horses on the back of a
truck. The ever busy François is supervising a group of
villagers as they attempt to erect a flagpole. When the
pole topples François scurries out of the way and ducks into
a nearby house, appearing almost immediately at the upstairs window just as the flagpole crashes through the porch
roof. One sees here, in François' sudden ability to dart
out of trouble's way, a character trait that will be carried
on to Hulot. One of the recurrent images in Les Vacances
is Hulot's head appearing at his attic window shortly after
he has caused some disaster. François learns to leap on
and off his bicycle with lightning speed. He does not even
take the time needed to stop and sort his mail; he simply
rides behind a moving truck, sorting his mail on the truck's
tailgate. His crazed exuberance causes him to peddle
straight through the middle of a bonfire; he also ends up de-
livering the mail into the most unusual of places.

     François' carnival-like abandon ends in disaster when
he finally crashes into a ditch. Soothed by an old woman
who knows that too much excitement can be a dangerous emotion, François feels ashamed and admits, like all morning-
after penitents, "I got excited." We see François back in

the field, helping with the haying, a sadder but wiser man.
The film ends as gently as it began with a small child following behind the carnival truck as it tows away the wooden
carousel horses.

The film was generally well received by both the public and the critics. One of the main criticisms of the film
was that it ran too long for the amount of material presented. Philip Strick cites The News Chronicle's reviewing the
film as "slapstick in the two-reeler Mack Sennett tradition."[38]
Strick goes on to recount:

> The Mail put forward the opinion, 'After a dullish
> forty-five minutes, which are presumably there to
> make the thing last the regulation hour and twenty,
> the picture spurts into a wildly funny slapstick se-
> quence.'[39]

Tati's style and choice of subject matter caused dissension
among critics as he moved into films of greater length.
Short films can more easily contain the rambling, plotless,
exploratory style of Tati. In expanding a short film into a
feature, as with Jour de Fête, the problem of structure became all the more obvious.

Georges Sadoul recognized the story weaknesses and
felt more emphasis should have been placed on the background of the village. "But the character he creates," Sadoul wrote, "unquestionably has life; he is very near to in-
stituting a type."[40] The strength of the film lies both in its
gags and in its character of François. Time magazine described Tati's character as "a sad-faced, gangling, rural
postman who looks like a cross between General Charles De
Gaulle and old-time silent comic Charles Chase."[41] Philip
Strick put his finger on a character trait that is as true for
Hulot as it is for François: "He is a lonely clown without
being pathetic...."[42] Tati's characterizations do not evoke
the same responses as Chaplin's, for example, who can be
just as pathetically down and out as he can be inspirationally
resourceful. We are not allowed by Tati to look too deeply
into the character of either Hulot or François. In Jour de
Fête, François is, also, too fast-moving to be pinned down
and analyzed.

Opposite, top: François the postman in an unusually calm
state of mind; bottom: François supervises the raising of
the village flagpole. Jour de Fête (1949). (Both courtesy
Academy Library.)

Dilys Powell has written in the London Sunday Times
that "this brilliant comedian has restored something almost
lost from the screen: the joke made to your eyes...."[43]
Powell goes on to describe the split-second timing of each
gag, the turning back on itself of a gag after it appeared to
be heading in another direction, and the quirks and subtleties anyone catches on to after a second and third viewing.
Strick takes delight in pointing out "the incidental touches,
evidence of a Keatonish awe of the potencies of the inanimate...."[44] The distant rattle of the cowbell on the handle-
bars, the apples that rain down upon François when he rides
straight into a tree, the mailbag that swings in circles a-
round the shoulders and the bell rope that continually lifts
people into the air when they try to pull it are all the small
touches that combine to form the unique flavor of the film.

Tati's gags, as often as they may be compared to
Chaplin, are essentially different. Chaplin was not averse
to using a certain maliciousness in order to get a laugh.
Tati's gags, in accordance with his filmic character, were
softer, more tolerant of others. As Strick has pointed out,
"the unfortunate squinter becomes, under François patient
guidance, an asset to the community, whereas Chaplin would
have subjected him to all kinds of mockery."[45]

Strick has quoted C. A. Lejeune in an effort to dif-
ferentiate between the slapstick themes of Jour de Fête and
a quieter, more documentary theme:

> To my mind the film was weakened by a conflict
> between two styles: the frank knockabout and the
> comedy of character. It begins and ends with a
> delicate impression of a small French town on a
> fair day. All the rest is slapstick, good slapstick
> admittedly, but not what the picture promised, and
> when all the fun is over I was left regretting a
> lost 'jour de fête.'[46]

Lejeune's sense of conflicting elements is felt by few other
critics. Tati's carefully created locations and atmosphere
for each of his films becomes, in fact, an addition and not
a distracting or conflicting element. It is the pastoral gen-
tility of the village of Ste.-Sévère as opposed to François'
frenzied activity that makes both François' change of character and the slapstick gags all the funnier. In subsequent
films Tati will painstakingly establish atmosphere for the
purposes of juxtaposition. Hulot's harried behavior stands

out all the more against the lazy resort hotel of Les Vacances. The comparison of colors, sounds, architecture and
general pace of life between the old quarter and the new
quarter in Mon Oncle is essential to the film. The juxtaposition of moods is essential to the inter-cut sequences of
Trafic. And Playtime, of course, relies greatly upon the
cold and disorienting landscape of modern Paris.

        Tati's technical handling of Jour de Fête was similar
to the straightforward approach of many early silent clas-
sics. Strick has quoted Matthew Norgate's observation:

        It is the absence of close-ups, coupled with a com-
        plete indifference to lighting and any particular re-
        gard for modern ideas of camerawork that makes
        Jour de Fête reminiscent of the silent days. [47]

Tati's apparent de-emphasis of technical aspects, outside of
sound, would continue to be characteristic of his films.

        In retrospect, one is able to look back upon Jour de
Fête and note the absence of certain elements that have
since become mainstays of Tati's work. The use of sound
in the film is less inspired than in his later films. As was
stated in reviews of the day, the film is better seen than
heard. There are, however, exceptions within the film that
can be seen as harbingers of Tati's audio expertise. The
scene where François is attacked by a wasp on a country
road is a strong sound gag. We hear the wasp's buzzing but
never see it and, although François' visual antics add to
the comedy, it stands essentially as a sound gag. Jour de
Fête is one of only two Tati films that has subtitles and it
is the only film that really needs them. A year after its
1950 release in England, Tati chose to reissue the film and
to employ a narrator to help explain part of the action.
Jacques Pils, who narrates in French-accented English, is
particularly effective when, at the close of the film, he mentions that the fair comes to the village but once a year. It
seems a blessing that the village and especially poor François are spared this event happening any more often.

        Fred Orain, Tati's producer, put forward the plan
that the film be shot in a new color process known as
"Thomson-Color." The use of color as an expressive element was one of the intended improvements over the earlier
short film. The process failed almost disastrously. Fortu-
nately, there had been a black-and-white safety print made,

as well, and it is because of that safeguard that the film
exists today. It was not until Mon Oncle, a decade later,
that Tati was again able to work with color.

When the film was completed distributors turned it
down. It simply did not fit into any of the categories of the
day. No one was going to take a chance on such an eccentric piece of work. It is necessary to have a sense of the
postwar French cinema in order to fully appreciate the impact a film such as this made. Spurred on by René Clément's film on the Resistance movement, La Bataille du
Rail, completed just a few months after the war ended,
French cinema adopted the war and resistance film as its
mainstay. Sadoul has pointed out "between 1945 and 1948
record box-office takings were recorded principally by war
films."[48] An "intimate realism," following in the tradition
of the pre-war work of Renior, threaded its way into the
fabric of French cinema. But, as Sadoul was quick to add:

> Commercial timidity caused French film producers
> to scurry quickly back to time-worn, proven sub-
> jects and to deal with harshly contemporary sub-
> ject matter no further than what they were allowed
> during the occupation.[49]

This "intimate realism" concerned itself with the family unit
and its day-to-day activity. No explorations were made, as
in the Italian Neorealism, of man in connection with his society. There had been relatively little comedy since the
days of the silents. The Prévert brothers had produced
L'Affaire Est dans le Sac, Adieu Léonard and Voyage Surprise, all respectable attempts at comedy. Voyage Surprise
even reintroduced the slapstick chase. But, as Sadoul points
out, either a forced liveliness or bitter sarcasm spoils the
mood of these films. It was into just such a setting that
Tati dropped his François. The reactions from the critics
were what one would expect. The New York Times commented on Jour de Fête's 1952 release in America:

> Since the French movie men have acquired an hon-
> est reputation for suave comedy, it must be ex-
> plained that they may upset all previous concep-
> tions with Jour de Fete, which makes a complete-
> ly unseemly bid for the mantle of Mack Sennett.[50]

Roy Armes, in his French Cinema Since 1946, describes Tati's first feature as one that is isolated from the

body of French cinema of the 1940's.   He places the film
in this context:

> It heralded no new school of comedy and four
> years passed before another film of Tati's appear-
> ed, but Jour de Fête was sufficient to mark out
> its director and star as one of the most original
> talents in the history of the French cinema. [51]

Tati's position in the world of cinema has always
been outside of any categories.   With the predominance of
French cinema of the 1930's behind them and the New Wave
of the late 1950's yet to appear, Tati landed with his eccentric offerings into an industry lacking identity.   Both his
sporadic output and his singular brand of filmmaking have
caused a tendency to speak of French cinema and Jacques
Tati as two separate things.

If the distributors were cool to Jour de Fête, the
public loved it.   Tati previewed it for enthusiastic audiences
who felt the plot, however, to be a little thin.   Tati and
producer Orain quickly wrote and inserted a few more gags,
such as François' bursting into a candlelit room and spout-
ing lighthearted pleasantries at a friend who appears to be
dressing for the carnival, without noticing there is a corpse
lying on the bed.   Tati also found it necessary to recut the
film, improving the tempo of the gags.   Tati finally got one
distributor to preview the new version at Neuilly.   The enthusiastic reaction meant a general release was soon to follow.   The film eventually won the prize for the best scenario at the Venice Film Festival in 1949 and won the Grand
Prix du Cinéma at Cannes in 1950.   With this film's success
Tati was able to promote his early short version, L'Ecole
des Facteurs, and win the Max Linder prize in 1949.

In characteristic style, Tati turned down offers to
make a sequel, although his financial backers were keen on
the idea.   It was suggested that François get married in a
film to be called Le Facteur Se Marié (The Postman Gets
Married) or that he go to Paris in Le Facteur a Paris.

CHAPTER 5

THE CREATION OF MR. HULOT

Although the postman had proved a gold mine, Tati's thoughts had already leaped beyond François to the creation of a character that would be considered universal. He wished to create a figure who could fit into nearly any background, unobstrusively, and therefore allow Tati more freedom in the choice of themes and story ideas. The character was to be, according to Philip Strick, a "twentieth century Everyman."[52]

One must realize that the costumes and very characters of the silent clowns were arrived at, to a great extent, intuitively. Chaplin hit upon the costume for his character as early as his second film. From that point Chaplin simply had to experiment to find what was inside the outline he had chosen. "Art is often something done before it is something thought,"[53] Kerr has observed. No one could believe that Langdon's innocent, baby-like character could have been formulated consciously. It was Lloyd's conscious approach to creating a character that caused him to first take the guise of the uninspired and unoriginal Lonesome Luke. Unlike Lloyd's copying of Chaplin, Tati's Hulot was a completely unique creation. It must be noted here that Chaplin, Keaton, Lloyd, Langdon and Tati all spent a certain number of years learning their trade before ever getting in front of a camera. They each shared a solid backlog of comedy gags, techniques, acrobatics, dance steps and more; all of which placed these special men on the same level as dozens of other well-trained film clowns. Inspiration was that final intangible that no amount of training or experience could provide. Chaplin may have come up with his Tramp very early; it took Lloyd nearly a hundred short films before he introduced his own inspiration: the "glasses character." Of course, the training these men went through was essential in filling out the form of their particular characters, but on-

40

ly after experienced intuition provided those characters.
The years on the stage, the experiments with short films
and the creation of François all gave Tati the tools needed
to exploit the character that his inspiration had provided
and called Hulot.

Tati, always observant of people's character traits,
knew a sergeant while in the army who was so good natur-
ed that it was impossible for any officer to stay angry with
the man for long.   From this man Tati started to get a
sense of Hulot.   An architect that Tati once knew became
the inspiration for Hulot's eccentric walk and inability to
choose the simplest course of action.   Tati has said that
"Hulot is not really a character.   He is just a fellow in the
road."[54]   But Hulot really is a character.   He is not as
eccentric as the little Tramp or the Stoneface, but he does
stand apart from society in his unique way.   It is not necessary for Hulot, or Chaplin or Keaton, to blend into the
masses in order to assume the role of an Everyman.   What
is required for any character to take on a universality is
that he project back to each person in the audience little
pieces of themselves.   Although Hulot, as comedy archetype,
is the very first character in any way like himself, there
exists a common bond between him and the rest of humanity.

Hulot's costume is not the absurdly assembled outfits
of the early silent clowns.   Hulot's manner of dress is almost totally unremarkable.   It is Hulot's style of walk that
sets him off immediately from other people.   Pitched forward, appearing almost to be on tiptoes, Hulot walks with
long determined strides.   He appears to be a man who knows
exactly where he is going; all the funnier because in fact
Hulot is never quite sure in which direction he should walk.
He may take a few tentative steps in one direction then realize he wants to head another direction, halt, reposition
himself and bound off on the new track.   Hulot's walk is so
resolute that he may very easily stride a few paces beyond
his destination before he even realizes where he is.   A running gag in Les Vacances is a gooey mass of taffy slowly
dripping off its taffy hook.   Several times Hulot saves the
taffy just before it drips to the ground.   A lovely comedy
bit shows Hulot, walking toward the hotel entrance, eyeing
the taffy suspiciously as he passes.   As the taffy starts to
drip downwards, Hulot continues walking past, all the while
noticing the taffy and wanting to spin around and save it.
Not until he has taken an extra two or three steps does Hu-

Hulot in <u>Playtime</u> (1967) (courtesy French Film Office).

lot manage a pirouette and rescue the drooping mess. At
another point in the film we see the vacationing Hulot, suitcases in hand, about to start up the stairs to his attic room.
Before he starts the climb he prepares himself by making
certain he is pointed in the right direction, raising himself
on tiptoe and finally lunging forward.

Hulot's costume, although it would go almost unnoticed on a less eccentric person, is assembled of humorously
disproportionate articles of clothing. He wears a crumpled
raincoat, far too short for his lanky figure, which sets off
his gangly legs even more, and he constantly carries an umbrella, rain or shine. It is as if he were warned years
ago that it might rain and does not want to be caught unpre-
pared. His pants are too short, revealing a section of absurdly striped socks beneath. Hulot usually wears a sporty
looking hat and often clenches a long-stemmed pipe in his
teeth, which muffles the occasional word he might speak.

Hulot's face is usually agreeably blank. Occasionally
a hidden look of panic may be detected behind his eyes.
Guilt, fear and a range of other emotions do somehow manage to surface and yet the expression seems never to change
on Hulot's face. It is as if Tati has created a face that
will mirror back to the viewer whatever emotion or state
of mind the viewer may be experiencing.

Silent comedy was first characterized by the wildly,
almost uncontrollably staged gags of Mack Sennett's characters. With the rise of the comedy greats a certain control
and finesse was brought to physical comedy. Max Linder
was perhaps the only well-known exception to the comedy
styles of the day. Linder preferred restraint in his gags
and avoided physical situations whenever possible. One
might easily wish to compare Linder to Hulot. However,
Hulot's physical relation to his world fell somewhere between Linder's reticence and Keaton's machine-oriented acrobatics. Hulot will scurry away from anything particulary
physical in the knockabout sense of comedy. Hulot tends
to become entangled in absurd situations that stand on a
different level from simple pratfalls: Hulot is not always
the center of the gag. Unlike Chaplin, Keaton and the
other classic clowns, Hulot may simply serve as the catalyst for many of the funny situations. He flips the switch
and then scuttles out of the way.

Hulot carries with him a certain amount of innate
guilt. When he finally becomes aware of the havoc he has
created, he becomes like a child who wants to run and hide.
When Hulot, in Les Vacances, fiddles with the line that
holds a sailboat up on its runners and accidentally sends
the boat sliding into the water, one sees the thoroughly
guilt-ridden Hulot pretending to stand nonchalantly by and
dry his back with a towel. Hulot does not realize that the
towel is looped around a pole behind him and that the mo-
tions of drying himself are all too apparently false. In
Trafic, Hulot is stuck upside down in a tree; in an effort
to go unnoticed he simply hangs there while his companions
talk below him. The unwarranted penitence Hulot displays
whenever he notices what he has done is incredibly funny.

Both François the postman and Hulot are rebels of
sorts. François rebelled against the pace of society, caused
his own brand of havoc and finally, like a comic Icarus,
fell to earth. Hulot's rebellion is simply to saunter through
life as a man, in Tati's own words, of "complete independence, of an absolute disinterest"[55] and whose own blundering is his principal shortcoming. Philip Strick commented
that Hulot was not the rebel the critics insisted he was but
simply a person who had trouble fitting in with society.
Despite his difficulties, Hulot always wanted to be a part of
society (somewhat unlike the speed-crazed François). But
pushing Hulot into his isolated position is the matter of his
special objectivity on the world. Hulot is intimidated by
the insanity he sees around him and is ready to bolt like a
frightened rabbit at the first scent of trouble. Hulot is a
victim of himself and even if he appears the rebel, he still
wants to belong to society.

Philip Strick has described the struggle within Hulot
as being between "the battle to keep up appearances" and
his tendency at "withdrawing into the tiny world of himself."[56] Strick points out that this turmoil is the problem
of every clown and that it is Hulot's impressive character
that makes him refuse to knuckle under and hide within himself. He is in fact amusingly relentless in pursuit of life.
He refuses to be left behind, even long after people have
amply demonstrated their dislike for him. There are two
coexistent universes: Hulot's and that of the rest of the
world. No one is able to share Hulot's universe with him.
He is not, however, totally cut off. Tati has created characters that are able to glimpse Hulot's world from a safe
distance and appreciate its special qualities. They are char-

acters that secretly root for Hulot. For any character to
openly root for Hulot would be too risky; that person might
easily become stranded with Hulot on the wrong side of the
fence. Martine, the young lady in Les Vacances, admires
Hulot and appreciates the gentlemanly attention he shows
her. The little old man who obediently follows his wife,
always walking the prescribed ten paces behind, is an excellent example of the man with responsibilities and commit-
ments admiring the man of freedom. The old man delivers
one of the very few lines of coherent dialogue in the film.
As the vacationers are leaving he bids Hulot a furtive goodbye, ever aware of his wife's gaze, and says, "We'll have
to meet sometime." To a character like Hulot, that is a
kind thing to say and well more than Hulot ever expected.

The very title of the film Mon Oncle implies some
sort of relationship. Little Gérard has a great affection
for his eccentric Uncle Hulot. It is this relationship that
spurs on much of the action of the film. Later, in Playtime, Tati will use a young woman tourist as Hulot's sym-
pathetic connection with the rest of the world. The people
who admire Hulot are so few because, in order to do so,
one must take a chance. Penelope Gilliatt has observed
that Hulot's "natural allies are mongrel dogs and dirty children who follow him in droves."[57]

Tati takes great pains to set Hulot off from the rest
of the world, not only in Hulot's perceptions but in his out-
ward behavior as well. Hulot arrives at the seaside hotel
in Les Vacances by car, everyone else arrives by train.
Hulot is the only one in costume at the hotel's masquerade
party. In Mon Oncle Hulot rides a bicycle while his relatives drive a shiny new car.

Tati has constructed Hulot along such simple lines
and with such simple motivations that Hulot's actions and
intentions are never complex. Hulot usually endeavors to
do no more than simply get from place to place. In Playtime he is trying to find the elusive Monsieur Giffard; in
Trafic he attempts to transport a camping car the 300 miles
from Paris to Amsterdam. In Les Vacances he simply
tries to take advantage of every activity the tiny resort has
to offer. Unlike the most dramatic schemes of Chaplin,
Keaton, Langdon or Lloyd, Hulot does not try to win the
girl, find true happiness or earn great honors. He simply
tries to get by, to be treated as just another person.

Hulot is decidedly less farcical than François. Tati
feels that Hulot is funny only in the way that everyone is
funny. Hulot does no more than reflect common patterns
of behavior. In designing Hulot as a more nearly "normal"
character, Tati intended that he fit in with any of the surroundings into which he was placed. One would have a difficult time imagining François in any setting other than his
small village. Roy Armes described François as so unrealistic a character that he does not always seem to fit in
with the other, more realistically drawn characters of his
village. Armes explained:

> This is one reason for Tati's refusal to make
> other films with this character, and Hulot is an
> attempt to create a character who will fit in bet-
> ter with his surroundings, whatever they may be.
> This integration is the inevitable outcome of Tati's
> attempt to make comedy more realistic. [58]

Tati attempts to demonstrate that the ridiculous things that
happen to Hulot are the things that can happen to anyone.
Tati's gags are rooted in reality and reveal more about
one's life than would some totally fantastical gag. Tati has
explained that "you have at least five minutes of Hulotism a
month--when you take the wrong seat on a train for example."[59]

Inherent in Tati's themes is Hulot as the Old World
gentleman. His manner of dress, his dignified demeanor,
his umbrella that serves as a walking stick all create the
sense of a character left behind from another era. Among
the cool and chic modern settings of Tati's last three films,
Hulot takes on the air of a symbolic relic, a reminder of
just how far society has come. Although Hulot displays the
manners of past generations, his insecurity, hidden behind
the gentlemanly facade, can often cause him to overdo the
role of the gentleman. He need not bow to others as often
as he does and, in general, he need not be so deferential.
A tiny moment in Les Vacances where Hulot greets people
on his way in to dinner illustrates this point. As he passes the glass partition into the dining room he nods, unthinkingly, at his own reflection. Hulot would be the perfect
gentleman if only he felt secure and did not need to go overboard in his actions.

Hulot does not display self pity or pain. If he is
rejected, he simply moves on to his next activity with un-

daunted enthusiasm. There is no pining away over lost
love, no rejection taken to the heart. It seems that everything, which would smite a normal person somehow rolls off
Hulot's back. Gerald Mast has said "he simply exists as a
sounding board for the rest of the activities in the film ...
he doesn't bounce back or react in any way."[60]

        Tati stresses that Hulot is a character who must per-
form his gags without realizing he is doing anything unusual.
When Hulot arrives at the Hôtel de la Plage in Les Vacances, he throws the front door open in order to carry in his
luggage. By allowing a stiff breeze then to blow through
the lobby, Hulot is disturbing everyone, unintentionally, before he has even met anyone. The tight-lipped hotel keeper
then storms over to kick the door shut but Hulot has just,
a moment earlier, closed the door and, unaware that he has
caused any trouble, proceeds toward the front desk. In a
beautifully staged scene later in the film Hulot is engrossed
in an energetic and noisy ping-pong game. When he goes
to retrieve the loose ball he disrupts a card game by swiv-
eling a man's chair out of his way. The man, staring at
his cards, is turned facing a new table of card players.
He lays down his cards into the wrong game. A melee follows over alleged cheating and Hulot, oblivious to anything
but his ping-pong game, goes peacefully on his way.

        When Hulot is not totally oblivious to what is going
on around him he is like someone who has just awakened
from sleep. He tends to be confused and disoriented, but
always with a look of propriety on his face similar to Langdon but with less innocence and a bit more uncertainty. Hulot handles many of life's simple tasks as if he had never
done them before. He has a quality of discovering his
world as he goes along; it is all an adventure, as if he were
in a foreign land. Humorously juxtaposed to this is the near
pathological professionalism he displays when he embarks on
any activity. Only Hulot would play a ping-pong game so
vigorously that he has to fade back a dozen feet from the
table in order to return the ball. Only Hulot would start a
game of tennis and become so engrossed in his lightning-
fast serve that he frightens everyone off the court.

        Hulot's lack of awareness is diametrically opposed to
the awareness with which Chaplin approached his own gags.
The scene in Les Vacances where Hulot's car tire, covered
with leaves, is mistaken for a funeral wreath is an elaborate gag which occurs accidentally. Hulot, in a sense, has

One of Tati's earliest pantomime routines reappears in Les
Vacances de Monsieur Hulot (1953). Hulot's eccentric but
powerful serves drive everyone off the court. (Courtesy
French Film Office.)

---

nothing to do with it. Had Chaplin been involved the character would have stuck the leaves to the tire for whatever reasons he might have had. Tati has illustrated the difference
with this story:

> Recently my wife was ill, she had a piece of pipe
> to put in her nose--it did not cure her, incidental-
> ly--and it looked like a piece of sausage. If this
> had happened in a Chaplin film, trying to make
> the pipe work, he would have taken a piece of
> bread and pretended to eat the pipe. Hulot could
> not do such a thing. He does not know things,
> they come to him. He is a fly-paper, he does not
> look for things. [61]

In line with this comparison goes a basic difference in story structure. In a Chaplin comedy Chaplin is the reason for the film. He must, almost always, be in the scene for it to have any more than a secondary relevance to the film. Hulot, on the other hand, need only pass through the scene. Entire sequences, especially in Tati's later films, work effectively even though they are minus Hulot. Tati has said of Hulot:

> He passes, he closes a door, you can not see
> him, it is for you to find him, it is for you to
> decide whether he is your friend or just someone
> you would not care to invite into your house. [62]

To talk of Chaplin's humor is to talk of the little Tramp. To talk of Tati's humor is to talk of much more than Hulot, who might best be considered as simply the thread that ties Tati's rambling comedies together.

André Bazin has written affectionately of Hulot, calling him "the genius of inopportunity."[63] Bazin sees in Hulot a special grace; "he is a scatter-brained angel, and the disorder he produces is that of tenderness and of liberty."[64]

It must be observed that while Hulot seemed to be a fully formed and complete character in his very first film, Les Vacances, Tati has conducted an almost unnoticed transformation of Hulot's character over the years. The Hulot one observes in the latest Tati film to date, Trafic, is less timid than the earlier Hulot. He is able to manage his crew of co-workers and gets the camper car all the way from Paris to Amsterdam. Although he manages to create problems along the way, he does manage to accomplish something that the earlier Hulot would have found overwhelming. Penelope Gilliatt has described Hulot as "agreeably unemployable."[65] In Trafic, Hulot is just the contrary: agreeably employed as an advertising and promotion man for the Altra car company. It is as if the Hulot one remembers in Mon Oncle and Playtime had come to terms, just slightly, with the world he had found so intimidating.

CHAPTER 6

LES VACANCES DE MONSIEUR HULOT

In the summer of 1951 in St.-Marc-sur-Mer, a small
Atlantic resort town in the province of Brittany, filming began on Tati's second feature, Les Vacances de Monsieur Hulot (Mr. Hulot's Holiday). Due to financial difficulties it
would not be until October of the following year that filming
would be completed.

Tati's approach to the filming was meticulous. Although the film was fully planned out before he arrived, Tati spent three months in the resort town--nearly converting
the tiny hotel into a studio--working out story ideas. The
film is simply the story of Monsieur Hulot and his annual
few weeks' vacation at a small, middle-class summer resort. The Hôtel de la Plage is filled with a wide variety
of vacationers, all of whom approach these precious few
weeks with the same regimented drive they bring to the rest
of their lives. Into this group arrives Hulot who, in his
own way, takes up the challenge to cram as much vacationing into the next few weeks as possible. What follows is an
almost nonstop series of gags which only subsides as the
tiny resort closes for the season and the vacationers head
back to the city.

The structure of Les Vacances is as simple as the
earlier Jour de Fête and quite similar. Both films are set
in sleepy rural locations, the authenticity of which gives
each film a documentary feel. Early sections of both films
are devoted to setting the lazy and relaxed mood of both
towns. Just as the annual traveling fair changes the mood
of the tiny farming village, so does the annual influx of
tourists change the mood of the sleepy seaside resort. Both
François and Hulot can be regarded as the very personifica-
tion of these annual changes of mood. After a series of

situations in which François or Hulot comically upsets the
existing order, the films each close with the departure of
the disturbance and a renewed calm. The structure of both
films is episodic, almost picaresque. One incident follows
another in random order. Like the links of a chain they
are interchangeable. Tati does not so much build his incidents, step by step, to a climax or a pay-off scene but,
rather, ends the films when he feels the audience has had
enough. While both François and Hulot may appear to be
changed men at the close of the film, Hulot is merely in a
temporarily subdued state and François, who has gained a
new knowledge, returns to his old pattern of behavior. Tati does not deal in character change. This episodic structure affords Tati the room he requires to stage his volume
of gags. Arthur Knight has commented that "ideas seem to
flow from Tati in a cataract. Like a cataract they are
rarely neat or tidy, but their effect is cumulative."[66] Just
as Fellini gathers together an assortment of memories,
ideas and jokes to create films with the structure of a simple scrapbook (Fellini: Roma, The Clowns, Satyricon), so
does Tati assemble his views of a certain location and activity and present them with a certain unstructured exuberance.

When Tati was asked why Les Vacances had so little
plot he answered:

> To me a simple man spending a fortnight at a
> lovely beach, a vacation for which he has saved
> his money all year, and to which he goes with
> his mind-set of having a good time--his is a
> great adventure to him and to all people who can
> understand his desires.[67]

There are, however, certain leitmotifs, in addition
to Hulot's presence, that serve to bind the film together.
The elderly man, following quietly behind his wife, will
suddenly appear from nowhere and, like a tiny funeral procession, march off into the distance. The repeated "ker-
plunk" of the dining room door as it swings open and shut
is a lovely sound gag and interlaces the entire film. A
cloud of pipe smoke followed by Hulot's guilty face popping
out of his attic window is a unifying element which follows
shortly after Hulot has caused some disaster.

Tati occasionally plunges into tangents which lead him
away from his loosely defined path. In one charming scene,

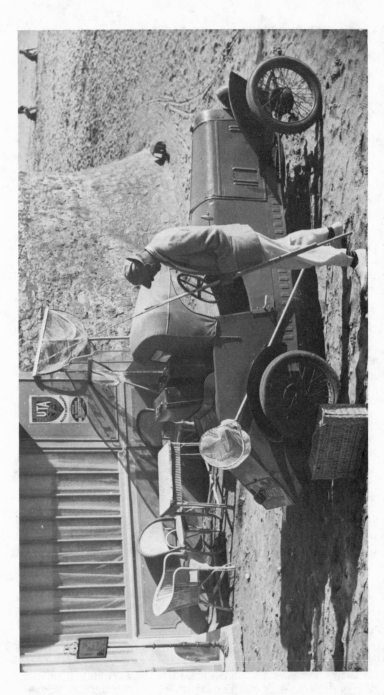

Hulot arrives at the hotel in Les Vacances de Monsieur Hulot (1953). (Courtesy French Film Office.)

a small boy buys two ice cream cones and, balancing them
carefully, struggles up a flight of stairs into the hotel dining room.   There he hands one of the cones to an even
smaller boy.   The two boys sit contentedly watching as decorations are hung for that evening's masquerade dance.
More than just charming, the scene works as a much-need-
ed pause in the breakneck pacing of Tati's gags.

A. J. Cauliez has described Les Vacances as a film
with a spatial feel to it as opposed to the temporal feel of
Jour de Fête's one day a year carnival.   Les Vacances is
full of displaced people; people in a foreign location who
adapt their patterns of behavior accordingly.   This spatial
orientation is a fundamental element in Playtime as well.
But Cauliez overlooks the temporal quality of Les Vacances.
The seaside resort is crammed with vacationers all trying
to pack as much "fun" and "relaxation" as possible into
their all too brief holidays.   This mood of the characters
almost frantically and unthinkingly hopping from one activity
to the next, with Hulot leading the way, is a mood grounded
in the sense that precious time is slipping by.

Tati introduces Hulot, his new film character, in a
unique manner.   One first hears Hulot's sputtering, backfiring 1924 Amilcar as it winds its way across the peaceful
Brittany countryside.   Hulot brings his absurd looking car
to a halt at a country crossroad where a lazy dog lies sun-
ning himself.   Although the dog has just moved out of the
way for another vehicle, he makes no such effort for Hulot.
In fact, the dog does not seem to notice Hulot's clanking
jalopy at all.   Although Hulot goes unseen, his tall frame
crammed inside the tiny car, one is already getting a sense
of his character through the personality of the car and the
silly situation with the lazy dog.   It is not until he arrives
at the hotel that one gets to actually set eyes upon Hulot.
By this time Tati has essentially introduced his character.

Although the gags in Tati's later films will share
their importance with the films' underlying themes, the gags
in Les Vacances are basically what the film has to offer.
As Hulot's eccentricity begins to take its toll among his
summer acquaintances, Tati will stage gags that do not directly involve Hulot but are, rather, reactions to Hulot.
In a wonderfully simple gag, one of the hotel keepers is
rolling up one of his shirt sleeves to retrieve a pen he has
dropped into an aquarium.   Disturbed by Hulot's presence,
the hotel keeper then plunges the wrong arm into the water,

soaking his entire sleeve.   In yet another gag that involves
minimal action one watches a waiter slicing roast beef.
Seen crossing the frame in the background is one of the hotel's skinnier guests.   The waiter slices a thin piece of
beef.   Then, as one of the fatter guests passes by, the
waiter slices off a thick piece of beef.   The gag is so sub-
tle that many people miss it.   Tati is here beginning to
develop a style of comedy that leaves much up to the perceptions of the viewer.   This approach to comedy will be
fully realized in Playtime, with the long shot encompassing
many activities at once and allowing one to construct one's
own movie.   Another gag from Les Vacances that leaves
much to the perception of the audience involves the constantly oozing taffy as it stretches closer and closer to the
ground.   The taffy is placed in close foreground in the
frame; Hulot passes by in the background.   The setup is the
same as the scene with the roast beef.   Depending upon how
one perceives the shot, one sees the taffy flowing downwards
and then catches Hulot's acrobatic attempts to save it.   Or
one overlooks the taffy and first sees Hulot walking past,
then sees his reaction and only then notices the taffy.   It
is as if Tati allows his audience to edit the scene themselves.

Hulot's battle with machinery, a larger theme in later films, is surfacing noticeably in this film.   Hulot's being
nearly swallowed by the collapsing kayak or letting his car
tire roll away are clear indications of the man's innocence
in a machine world.   Hulot is so poorly versed in the ways
of simple machinery that, in an attempt to quickly fill a watering can, he will run in circles behind a spinning sprinkler with the can extended up to the sprinkler's nozzle.   All
Hulot has to do, in reality, is to grab the sprinkler, stop
it from twirling in circles and fill the can.

Recurrent gags, some of which work as leitmotifs,
are an element Tati uses in Les Vacances probably more
than in any other film.   The ever dripping taffy is one.
The cacophony of Hulot's automobile is another.   Tati uses
some of his recurrent gags as pacing elements.   The sudden flipping on of lights in the darkened hotel in reaction to
some late night disturbance of Hulot's is used as a pause
after a string of gags.   The pompous voice of the announcer
on the hotel's radio is inserted into the film at ridiculous
moments, indirectly emphasizing the seriousness with which
these people take their lives.   Tati even constructs a recurrent gag and then fools the audience with it.   Hulot sits

quietly beside a record player, placidly smoking his pipe
and listening to a jazz record at a deafening volume.   The
irate hotel guests all storm into the room and turn off the
music; Hulot looks up innocently.   The same record is
heard at the same loud volume later in the film.   When the
guests again storm into the room they find, not Hulot, but
a little girl sitting by the record player, listening intently.

Arthur Knight has observed that "since mere form is
the least of Tati's worries, he often permits [the numerous
supporting players] little gags of their own...."[68]   As early
as Les Vacances one could sense Tati's de-emphasis of the
main character.   With Hulot absent from entire scenes, the
little boys with the ice cream cones, for example, one realizes Tati's comedy is distinct from that of the early film
clowns.   The first ten minutes of Les Vacances are spent
watching Hulot's eccentric car.   One can hardly imagine
Chaplin willingly surrendering an entire scene to the personality of a machine.   Even Keaton, whose penchant for machines was well known, would have chosen to interact with
the car in some way.   Tati's fascination with the small details of setting and action often makes the figure of Hulot unnecessary.   Although Hulot is the main character of Les
Vacances, this does not mean that the film is about him.
The boys with the ice cream cones, the boy on the beach
playing menacingly with his magnifying glass, the obedient
old man who tosses back into the ocean the seashells his
wife has just picked up, and the American businessman running for the phone--all these are amusing glimpses of Tati's
world that do not require Hulot's presence.

In addition, Tati brought to full realization in Les
Vacances something that would be an element in all his
films to come.   That is the telltale trail of disaster left behind by Hulot as he passes.   A perfect example is a scene
where Hulot enters the hotel lobby carrying a paddle, fresh
from his kayak accident.   Hulot's feet are covered with mud.
The hotel keeper notices the tracks across his clean floor
and follows them as they lead into the coat rack, under
which Hulot is hiding.   The coats on the rack shake with
fright.   When the hotel keeper turns his back for an instant,
Hulot bounds up the stairs, off camera.   The hotel keeper
looks around and now notices a trail of muddy footprints
leading up the stairs.   The camera reveals the top of the
stairway just as Hulot's kayak paddle is tossed into view and
slides down the stairs.   One sees only the signs of Hulot's
presence, muddy footprints, a discarded paddle but not the

character himself. In a scene where Hulot, the gentleman,
carries the young lady Martine's luggage into her cottage,
one watches as Hulot trips and stumbles out the backdoor
under the weight of the suitcases. Tati cuts to the back of
the house and shows Hulot stumbling in one side of the frame
and out of the other. Though Hulot has exited the frame,
one is still able to follow his progress. A long vine which
has tangled itself around the passing Hulot is stretched
tighter and tighter across the frame, a sign that he is
still on the move.

Another instance of onscreen evidence of an offscreen
Hulot is the early morning exercise class all doing knee
bends to the commands of an instructor. The group, grunt-
ing up and down in unison, suddenly comes to a halt in the
down position. They each hold this taxing position longer
and longer until it is obvious they can hold it no more.
Still no command comes from the instructor to straighten
up. The camera then reveals that Hulot has distracted the
instructor and is discussing some irrelevancy with him. Of
course, Hulot is unaware of the problem he is causing. Although the pay-off in this gag involves seeing what Hulot is
doing, most of the situation, the intriguing part, has Hulot's
offscreen presence determining the onscreen action.

When Hulot ignites a shack full of fireworks Tati,
again, displays the humor of Hulot's offscreen presence.
Tati shows Hulot's inept attempts to contain the fire, but
then goes to a distant long shot when the fireworks start to
explode. He allows one's imagination to create the scene
of Hulot running about, amongst the fiery holocaust, doing
whatever is inappropriate to stop it. One's own imagination,
given free reign, makes the scene funnier than if one actually watched Hulot. This style of presenting Hulot as an
offscreen personality as much as an onscreen personality
has been described in Newsweek magazine: "Jacques Tati is
a master of the fleeting appearance--glimpses of the loon."[69]
Tati's desire to spotlight a variety of other characters, as
much if not moreso than Hulot, will be called by Jonathan
Rosenbaum, Tati's "democratic comedy."

Hulot the man of mistrust for the physical world is
ever apparent in Les Vacances. What causes him to stumble when he carries young Martine's suitcases into her cottage is his mistaking a suitcase lying on the ground for the
top step of her porch. He steps onto it and is sent stumbling into her house and out the back door. When he climbs

the front steps again, watching carefully where he places his
feet, he extends his foot and tests midair as if whatever
tripped him up might now be invisible. One never knows.
When Hulot is served dinner he instinctively sniffs the knife
and bread as if he were a suspicious rabbit. When the
horse he attempts to ride reacts violently, he hurries to a
safe spot. Behind the bathhouse door, peering through a
small porthole cut in it, he observes the world like a frightened gopher peering out of its hole. The speed with which
Hulot retreats to his room after causing some minor disaster is an indication that the world has not been too gentle
on him. It is clearly to Hulot's credit and decidedly one of
his greatest traits that he so bravely sallies forth into the
world as often as he does.

Hulot's personal universe is so clearly and ruthless-
ly defined that he is cut off from most of the world. The
two hotel keepers simply stare suspiciously at him each
time he passes. Most of the guests nod their greetings, but
more out of a discomfort with Hulot than out of friendship.
Although Hulot's eccentricity may unnerve people, it can fascinate them, as well. When one of the stern-faced hotel
keepers sees Hulot making odd faces in the mirror, the man
joins in the action unconsciously, making faces of his own.
It is as if he wants to sample Hulot's madness and find out
what is going on inside that unusual head of his. When the
hotel keeper realizes what he is doing he comes to his senses and hurries away self-consciously. Hulot spends much
of his time discovering the world. He is like a creature
from another planet, totally unversed in life's conventions.
He will dawdle over the most commonplace things as if he
had never noticed them before. He has to be pointed in the
direction of the hotel dining room in order to find it. He
will do a simple action like walking through a door and then
pause and examine what he has just done, taking in the idea
of having walked through it. Hulot's point of view is fright-
eningly objective. He sees what everyone else overlooks
and is blind to what most people see.

Hulot, however, is not totally isolated by his personality. As discussed earlier, Tati has created characters
who secretly share a little of Hulot's madness. The little
old man admires Hulot's freedom. The young lady in the
film, Martine, feels some affection for him. In a scene
that was later removed, she bids Hulot a tender goodbye as
she leaves for home. A swarm of kids crowds around Hulot's car when he first drives up to the hotel. At the end

Hulot in the hotel dining room. <u>Les Vacances de Monsieur</u>
<u>Hulot</u> (1953). (Courtesy Academy Library.)

---

of the film, Hulot sits on a hill of dirt and wears the for-
lorn look of a scolded child. He and the group of kids play-
fully toss dirt at each other. He is accepted by the group
of ragamuffins on his own terms. But it becomes obvious
at this point that no one, regardless of their affection or affinity for Hulot, would surrender their place in this world
for a place in Hulot's.

In Hulot's exile from and suspicion for the rest of the
world he becomes a character swept by events along the path
of least resistance; he hops quickly and easily out of one ridiculous situation into the next. Tati's episodic structuring
of the film is dictated by this tendency of Hulot's. When
Hulot accidentally finds himself thrust in the middle of a funeral ceremony, he quickly blends into the reception line.
As he shakes hands and nods repeatedly at each of the de-
parting mourners, one realizes that only Hulot could allow
himself to be swept into such an absurd situation. When Hulot chivalrously offers to help a young lady carry her backpack, he does not realize that she is embarking on a hike up

a mountainside. Now caught up in this situation, he carries
her pack all the way to the top of the mountain. In Hulot's
frantic attempts to squelch the growing blaze in the fireworks shack, he will, as described earlier, chase a rotat-
ing sprinkler in circles in order to fill a watering can. In
order to locate the end of the water hose, Hulot will run
along the looped path of the hose, pirouetting with each loop,
until he comes to his destination. All one would need to do
is to look up and notice where the hose leads. But, for Hulot, the world is not to be trusted and things are not always
as they appear.

        Tati does not dig deeply into the souls of his charac-
ters. There are few moments of self-realization in his
films. Hulot, forlornly tossing clods of dirt at the band of
children, is about as close to Hulot's inner workings as one
will ever get. Tati deals with what a person reveals of
himself through his visible behavior, his actions. Tati does
not so much probe into people's lives as sit back and observe them from a fresh point of view. He is concerned
with what can be learned from watching people walk by on
the street. Tati, therefore, does not operate on the level
where dialogue is necessary. When appearances tell all it
is only required that "the characters merely start to say
something so obvious that it needs no finishing."[70] If Tati
is to observe the people on the street, it becomes necessary
that he cast his films with that in mind. Tati will, throughout his career, draft civilians into his films. He feels
there is no effective way to untrain a professional actor so
he works, in part, with whatever untrained people fit the
roles. Tati has said:

> In Mr. Hulot's Holiday I had some actors, but
> most of the people were just at the seaside resort
> in Brittany. I prefer that everyone should seem
> as natural as possible and as serious as possible
> about what they are doing. It is for us in the
> picture to be serious, for the audience to laugh.[71]

Nathalie Pascaud, who played the young lady Martine, was
merely a social acquaintance of Tati's. When Pascaud's
husband objected to her playing a part in the film, Tati, realizing the man was perfect for the role of the American
businessman, offered him the part. He accepted and was
eventually used to play Monsieur Arpel in Mon Oncle, as
well.

Alain Romans composed the lightly romantic musical score for Les Vacances. The main theme, which later became a popular hit in France, is a lightly captivating chanson. Romans' score manages to enhance the lazy and summery mood of the film. Tati chose to motivate the source of music in many places in the film: a distant radio or a phonograph in a window. The 1962 re-release of Les Vacances finds the film's delicate theme crushed beneath a more contemporary, jazz-oriented arrangement. Romans has stated that Tati was concerned with the film's seeming out of date: "Tati urged me to jazz up and bring up to date the score despite my advice.... He is very headstrong!"72 Tati also chooses to play long passages without music. Where a more conventional film would employ some underlying theme or rely on musical accentuations, Tati will often allow natural sounds to play.

Tati finds, in the natural sounds of the world, a music of its own. He is a master of the expressive sound effect; the first gag in Les Vacances is a sound one: the train station loudspeaker's blaring out a totally incoherent announcement. The sputtering and backfiring of Hulot's car, as he comes and goes throughout the film, seems a parallel to the distant tinkling of François' bicycle bell in Jour de Fête. The swinging door to the hotel dining room has a personality all its own due to its distinctive sound. Tati deals with the sounds, props and physical paraphernalia of a story as ends in themselves. To Tati, they may, indeed, be the story. Like Hulot, Tati concerns himself with the things that most people no longer see or hear. If a man is to walk across a room, it is not the purpose of his walk that Tati is concerned with, but rather the way the man moves and the sounds of his footsteps. One must here realize that the main character, Hulot, is responsible for all the loud sounds in the film. Juxtaposed with the soothing lull of the ocean waves are the sounds of a noisy ping-pong game, a blaring phonograph, or Hulot's car roaring off on some mission. At the close of the fireworks scene, after Hulot has awakened the entire hotel, a calm again settles on the night. But, to this sweet silence Tati sensitively adds the sound of a distant barking dog, the very dog that bothered Hulot earlier. The quality of silence is heightened or pointed out by the sound of the lone dog.

As with his earlier films, Tati's use of the camera is straightforward. He chooses to use static camera setups with only occasional moves to simply follow the action. Ta-

ti shoots no close-ups at all. He feels an audience should
not be directed to what to laugh at in a comedy. The audience must construct the film itself, choosing to look at or
ignore what it will. Consequently, Tati uses a wide-angle
staging of his scenes. The scene at the train station, early in the film, is filmed in a static, high and wide angle,
showing the entire station platform. This entire gag, showing a group of vacationers hurrying from one platform to
another, could almost have been presented on stage.

In accordance with Tati's appreciation for wide angle
staging is his use of backgrounds. Martine looks out her
window at the beach below. Two beach tents are being set
up, a man inside each one, struggling with it; the effect is
produced of two monsters wiggling on the beach. A man
walks along the beach exercising and kicking his legs high
into the air. The odd combination of activities seen below
is funny because the camera's wide angle lets one perceive
all the events simultaneously. This entire scene is played
as a background to the scene with Martine. In films to follow Tati would continue to exploit the potential of the background. The bustling nightclub in Playtime reveals many
planes of activity, as do the crowded garage scenes in Trafic.

Tati's editing and pacing is rudimentary in Les Vacances. It is the sheer volume of excellent gags that carries the film. There are, however, places in the film that
warrant a pause or a break from the action. Scenes that
may appear to be tangents leading away from the fast paced
action serve, in reality, as these much needed pauses. The
boys with the ice cream cones, Martine unpacking her suitcases, long shots of the dark and peaceful hotel at night all
serve as these pacing elements.

Tati has difficulty in this film orienting the audience
to the correct passage of time. He uses the simple technique of showing the hotel at night to tell the audience that
another day has passed. Tati did not have to handle the
passage of a considerable period of time in the earlier Jour
de Fête, whose story runs its course in just two days' time.
Playtime, likewise, takes place in a single day and Trafic
covers only two days. In Les Vacances, as one watches the
group of vacationers at dinner, Tati cuts to the road outside
to show the band of boys heading for the beach. He then
cuts quickly back to the front door of the hotel where the
vacationers are now seen posing for a group photo. The

sense of time Tati creates here is too brief to have moved
the people from their dinner to the outside of the hotel.
The scene where Hulot helps carry Martine's luggage inside
is followed too quickly with the shot of his driving down the
road. These elemental pacing and time orientation problems
seem to be a result of Tati's nonlinear, piecemeal film construction.

Upon completion of Les Vacances de Monsieur Hulot,
some of Tati's financial backers were gravely concerned with
the film's marketability. One of the financiers went so far
as to ask Tati if he actually planned to release the film.
Once again a public preview screening proved a convincing
factor; the screening at Châtenay-Malabry delighted the audience. The film proved reasonably successful in Paris when
first released in the early summer of 1953. Later that
summer, France underwent a general strike which closed,
among many things, the railroads. That was not so good
for Parisians who could not get away for their annual August
vacations. For Tati it proved a blessing. Stranded in Paris, a great many more people went to see the film than one
could have hoped for. Janet Flanner in her "Letter from
Paris" appearing in The New Yorker, described Tati "as
the man who during the strikes generously showed French
vacations as something Parisians should be glad they had
to miss."73 The film played for a number of weeks to ca-
pacity crowds.

If the normally dialogue-oriented French took well to
the film, the Americans made it a triumph. In the U.S.
the film rapidly became the number one revenue producing
film from France that year. The film won the International
Critics Award at Cannes in 1953, the Louis Delluc Prize in
1953, the Algerian Critics Prize and a special honor from
the French Federation of Ciné-Clubs.

CHAPTER 7

MON ONCLE

Tati first came to America in the fall of 1954 to promote Mr. Hulot's Holiday. He appeared on American television, N.B.C.'s "Fanfare," where he performed a number
of his stage pantomimes. Included were the tennis player,
soccer goalie and the fisherman. Tati had to emphasize
that none of the characters he was doing were Hulot and in-
dicated that Hulot was a character reserved for the screen.

Tati began nine months of shooting on Mon Oncle (My
Uncle), his third feature, in September 1956. The film was
not released until 1958, after a full year of editing and
sound dubbing. If Tati's first two features can be viewed
as reflections of classic silent comedy, then Mon Oncle can
be considered, as Cauliez has described, "pure Tati."[74]
Tati had brought into full focus the themes that would characterize his films from that point on. His comedy gags had
taken on a fully personal style. Tati was able, here, to
shoot in color and work with a much larger crew than he
had ever worked with. Along with the increased scope of
the film came certain new responsibilities. Tati recalls
that

> The presence of forty technicians ... waiting pa-
> tiently for a dog to deign to relieve himself along
> a gas burner put upon me great financial respon-
> sibilities.[75]

The film clearly sets up two opposing forces: Hulot
and his slowly-paced, oldfashioned values versus the chic
and ultra-modern values of his sister, Madame Arpel, and
her family. The film opens with a title sequence that seems
immediately to spell the doom of Hulot's fragile Old World
life-style. Drills and construction equipment pound away in
a cacophony much the same as the auto assembly plant that

63

was to open Trafic. Mon Oncle brings into prominence Tati's growing social awareness. Philip Strick has observed
that Tati has progressed from an "instinctive" satire to a
more conscious propaganda. In mentioning Mon Oncle,
Strick has written of a "doctrinary awareness behind nearly
every shot."76

        Hulot is represented in the film as a character with
some roots. Living in the old quarter of Paris, surrounded
by people whose values are similar, Hulot no longer seems
the hopeless loner presented in Les Vacances. In characteristic style, Hulot marches forth into the part of the world
he finds foreign, that is, the home of his relatives, the Arpels. Tati's move to identify Hulot with a community can
be seen as an attempt to make Hulot represent more than
simply himself.

        Cauliez has written that Mon Oncle leaves behind the
spatial or distance changes of Les Vacances and the temporal changes of Jour de Fête and shows that simple freedom
and the joy of life can be found in one's everyday environment. Tati has grounded his themes a bit more closely on
reality by taking Hulot out of an artificial or temporary environment and bringing him home.

        The film's storyline is, again, quite simple, but with
a few additions. Hulot, Madame Arpel's eccentric brother,
is unemployed, either by circumstance or by choice. The
Arpels lead a modern, efficient and "perfectly regulated
life."77 Madame Arpel busies herself delightedly with the
mass of modern appliances that fill her spotlessly clean,
but coldly sterile home. When guests drop in she babbles
on like a tour guide as she points out her appliances. Monsieur Arpel drives off each morning in his shiny new car to
the plastics factory where he oversees the production of
miles of plastic tubing. Gérard, the Arpel's nine-year-old
son, prefers the world of dirt piles, rough-and-tumble
games, barking dogs and other boys his age. Gérard finds
his parents' lifestyle wearisome. In short, he is on Hulot's
side of the fence. Gérard's affection for his uncle, like the
affinity felt by the gang of kids in Les Vacances, is easily
understood. It is through Gérard's eyes that one sees the
film. Hulot has opened up to his nephew an appreciation
for the simple and real values in life. Both Madame and
Monsieur Arpel have somewhat different ideas on education
and are clearly jealous of Hulot's influence over their son.
Arpel decides that Hulot should get a job. After Hulot fails at

Hulot gives his nephew Gérard (Alain Bécourt) a ride home from school. Mon Oncle (1958). (Courtesy French Film Office.)

---

one attempt at work, Arpel decides to give his brother-in-law a chance at the plastics factory. Hulot unfortunately inhales too much of some chemical fumes, grows drowsy and falls asleep on the job. He awakens to find the plastic tubing oozing from the machine in the irregular shape of a string of sausages. Arpel is furious and seeks a way of shunting Hulot off once and for all. In the meantime, Ma-

dame Arpel is attempting to link her hapless brother up with
one of her lady friends.   At a chic cocktail party, given one
afternoon by the Arpels, Hulot makes a concerted effort to
fit in with the other guests.   He starts to recount various
amusing stories but goes overboard when he tells an off-
color joke.   Madame Arpel's lady friend is offended.   Arpel
finally finds a job for Hulot in the provinces.   Hulot docile-
ly agrees and is packed off on the train, leaving Gérard and
his relieved father together.   When Arpel accidentally drives
into a streetlamp on the way home, one sees a similarity
between this and one of the rough games Gérard plays with
his friends.   Arpel and Gérard are able to laugh together.
It seems as if Hulot's influence has given Arpel some perspective on his life and has indirectly brought father and son
closer together.

Again Tati employs running gags that link the film's
activities together.   Gérard's game of distracting passers-by
by whistling at them at just the right moment to send them
walking into lampposts is a recurrent gag that is paralleled
by Arpel's accident with the lamppost at the close of the
film.   Hulot's pruning of a tree that Gérard has accidentally
broken a branch off of is another running gag.   Madame Arpel's front yard fish sculpture works as another gag interlac-
ing the film.   She hurries to turn on the water-spitting fish
whenever an important person arrives.   She turns the water
on for Hulot, mistaking him for someone else, only to dis-
gustedly turn it off again.

Tati has elevated the importance of the settings in
Mon Oncle to a level equal to that of the characters.   The
actual physical settings become characters of their own.
Tati even gives the settings gags to play.   The ramshackle
building that Hulot inhabits has a distinctive personality.
The building is dominated by its set of stairways that Tati
only allows one to glimpse from outside, through the windows.   The inside of the building, in fact, is never revealed
until the end of the film.   Through the windows Tati shows
his audience only bits of his characters' bodies.   Glimpses
of hands or a pair of feet are seen, nothing more.   Hulot's
feet, seen through the windows in one scene, appear on the
stairway landing.   A section of a woman, covered in a bath
towel, appears at a nearby window.   Hulot's expressive legs
tell us that he sees the woman, hesitates before going down-
stairs and finally does so as the woman scurries across the
hall.   The actions seen through the many windows take on a
multi-screen or split screen effect.   Tati in effect separates

his frame into many smaller frames and relates them to
each other. Penelope Gilliatt has commented:

> Tati is visually very interested in bits of people.
> If he were playing the game of pinning the tail on
> the donkey, I think he would tend to find the dis-
> sociated tail too engrossing to go any further. [78]

If the personality and charm of Hulot's habitat swings
one end of the film's seesaw, the stylish sterility of the
Arpel's house weighs down the other. The Arpels take
great pride in their stylized home. Their electronic garage
door, which has two portholes cut in it for windows, opens
and closes automatically as an infrared beam is cut. The
Arpels get locked in their garage when a roaming band of
dogs runs across the beam and sends the door shut on them.
Monsieur Arpel runs to one of the round windows, Madame
Arpel to the other. Their heads appear to be the pupils in
a monstrously large pair of round, rolling eyes. The setting, very obviously, becomes the subject.

The geography within the film becomes an expressive
element, as well. Between the modern quarter of town and
Hulot's old quarter stretches a barren area best described
as a terrain-vague or a no-man's-land. Here, in this area
of dirt and rubble, roams Gérard and his companions, a
typically Tati-esque assortment of dogs and small children.
This no-man's-land is a perfect and simple visual demarcation between the two worlds, Old and New. It is appropri-
ate that these two opposing forces have relinquished this
wasteland to the children. Children have not constructed
the allegiances or value systems of their parents. They
simply respond to whatever is human and real, regardless
of social acceptability. Hulot, to whom these kids feel an
automatic affinity, comes in contact with this motley crew
whenever he crosses from his world into the world of his
relatives. This area takes on a special, almost cherished,
significance for Hulot. He very carefully pauses to replace
a dislodged brick from an old wall as he passes.

The no-man's-land serves as a demarcation between
color schemes as well as between lifestyles and sensibili-
ties. With the exception of Jour de Fête, the color pro-
cessing of which was a complete failure, Tati here uses
color for the first time. He gives the old quarter of town
a warm feeling by using pastel pinks, greens and oranges
in both settings and costumes. The new quarter is repre-

Hulot surveys uneasily the Arpel's stylish front yard. _Mon Oncle_ (1958). (Courtesy Academy Library.)

Hulot (left) struggles his way along the Arpel's stylish side-
walk with Monsieur Pichard (Lucien Frégis, front) and Monsieur Arpel (Jean-Pierre Zola). Mon Oncle (1958). (Courtesy Academy Library.)

---

sented by harsher tones of green and electric yellow all juxtaposed to the sterile tones of beige, grey and white. Tati
included the costumes within the film's color scheme, as
well. He chose an appropriately harsh and gaudy red for
the costume of Madame Arpel's rather unbearable lady
friend. Cauliez feels Tati's use of color relates to more

than underlying themes: Tati's "comic colors"[79] effectively
heighten the humor in certain gags.

Gérard, whose spirit is straining to run free, is
treated by his mother as little more than another appliance.
The model home must have one of everything, including a
little boy. When Hulot allows Gérard to eat a deliciously
greasy doughnut before dinner, Madame Arpel does not allow her boy's contaminated fingers to touch the dinner she
has meticulously prepared for him. Madame Arpel domi-
nates her household as if it were the only meaningful thing
in her life. She is profoundly out of touch with the coarser
realities of life. When she spots a dead leaf lying in one
of the flower beds she is beside herself. When she boils
Gérard an egg she must first put on a pair of antiseptic
gloves before going through an absurdly complicated proce-
dure. The Arpel's idea of an evening at home is huddling
in the darkness around the faintly glowing television. The
Arpels have not only constructed an antiseptically cold environment in which to live, but have made the mistake of
assuming it to be the only way in which one should live.
Penelope Gilliatt defined the problem that faces the Arpels:

> The Arpels, who rather grow on you, are funny
> partly because they treat themselves as if they
> were machines and partly because they have lost
> the defining human sense of relative importan-
> ces.... They have no grasp of their scale in the
> universe. [80]

It is against this narrow-mindedness and lack of emotion
that Hulot demonstrates, by his example, the more essential values of life. If the Arpels choose to huddle in the
darkness about the television set, then Hulot enjoys sitting
around with a group of friends and singing. If a misplaced
leaf is too much for Madame Arpel to contend with, then
Hulot thrives on the disorderliness that is the by-product of
living.

The demands that Tati places upon Hulot are greater
in Mon Oncle than in the earlier Les Vacances. If Hulot is
actually to have an effect on little Gérard and his father,
then something more than the comically ineffectual Hulot of
before is required. Penelope Houston observed:

> Relationships are factors that Tati has not yet
> really tried to handle.... Tati, perhaps, would

like to humanize Hulot, to show him not as a catalyst setting off a comic reaction, but a man
with his own convictions. But there is something
in his personality that resists the human encoun-
ter. [81]

The detachment Hulot exhibits in his relationship to much of
the world's insanity is, perhaps, the same detachment he
shows in his relationships with people. Although there is
little doubt that Hulot loves his nephew, he maintains a cool
shell of propriety and unemotional calmness which keeps him
at a distance from the boy. What is important is that Gérard loves his uncle and senses, in the instinctive way of
children, that his uncle loves him.

Cauliez has compared Mon Oncle to the films of Italian neorealism. Just as neorealism explored the drama
and meaning in the smaller, commonplace moments of life,
so Tati satirizes everyday actions and events. Neorealism
offers its direct message by holding a mirror up to life;
Tati's message comes indirectly, as a result of his comedy.
Even Chaplin, in his later, more socially conscious comedies, did not subordinate the message to the comedy as
much as Tati has done. Whenever Chaplin carried a banner,
one was aware of it. Tati's banner is well concealed; the
power of the message is not noticed. It nevertheless hits
its marks: absurd social conventions, the dissipation of
man's control over his technology, an increasing isolation
from nature and the loss in human values.

Penelope Houston would not agree that Tati's films
go much beyond simple laughter:

He has no comment to make outside his own clearly defined limits. His comedy does not expand or
spread itself into generalization: it takes a series
of jokes and plays with them. ... But Mon Oncle
is his most substantial film precisely because Tati has begun to look at the world a little sadly; and
this has always been a quality of the gentle humor-
ists. [82]

Although there was a certain sadness in the characters of
Les Vacances, along with a feeling of pity and affection for
the isolated Hulot, the relationship between Hulot and Gérard
in Mon Oncle is more poignant. Tati is able to establish a
quiet and tender understanding between uncle and nephew. One

must have the sensitivity of Gérard to realize that Hulot has a great deal of love for the world. Hulot does manage to express his feelings, but only to those with whom he feels a certain safety: Martine in Les Vacances, Barbara in Playtime, and Gérard in Mon Oncle.

Hulot's silent love for the world is symptomatic of the tenderness with which Tati views humanity. Even the narrow-minded Arpels, as keen as they are on ridding themselves of Hulot's unsettling influence, are shown with sympathy and understanding. Hulot never considers them his enemy even if the story structure says he must. As discussed earlier, there are no villains in Tati's films, just people one does or does not admire. Tati has said: "I like Mon Oncle very much; it conducts (if you like definitions) a sort of defense of the individual, seen in a basically optimistic way."[83]

In accordance with Tati's slow pace of production, the cutting and dubbing of the film lasted nearly a year. Tati has always approached the editing of his films very simply, rarely using the cutting of a sequence to enhance a gag. Tati's editorial style has been noted by Penelope Houston:

> It is edited with an autocratic disregard for appearance or effect. The big central party sequence ... would in other hands have built to a toppling height of fantasy. Tati lets the scene dawdle, revives it, becomes fascinated with the mechanics of a joke, lingers on an irrelevancy. His sense of timing, it sometimes seems, is not so much erratic or individual as virtually nonexistent. Yet this take it or leave it confidence is fundamental to his whole approach to the cinema. In a machine age it becomes immensely attractive.[84]

Just as the use of wide-angle framing allows Tati the space he requires to perform his gags, so his slowly-paced editorial style gives him the time. Tati seems to resist the encroachment of technique--that is, anything technical--over the simplicity and straightforwardness of his ideas.

As usual, Tati insists that the dialogue in Mon Oncle be treated as a sound effect, blended into the careful symphony of sounds that characterize his films. The small talk,

idle chatter and tiny pleasantries that constitute much of people's dialogue is reduced to its actual importance, that of
sound. What matters to Tati is not so much what his characters say as the way in which they express themselves.
Madame Arpel's constant chatter is juxtaposed to the silence
of her brother, Hulot. The nervously incessant talk of the
young woman, Maria, in Trafic is more important in style
than in content. One does not need to decipher the excited
babble of the lady tourists in Playtime, the vacationers in
Les Vacances or the cocktail party guests in Mon Oncle in
order to appreciate what Tati is doing. Tati's unique point
of view allows his audience to see just how much of human
communication is little more than noise. When Hulot re-
counts his off-color story at the Arpels' cocktail party, Tati does not allow the audience to hear what is being said.
One simply watches the reactions of the guests to what Hulot is saying. One, then, quickly assumes that Hulot's un-
heard dialogue was a bit less than delicate. It must be remembered that Tati's background is that of a pantomimist
and stage performer who relies upon physical comedy in
which dialogue, humorous or otherwise, was never necessary.
It is natural that Tati would carry his dialogue-free humor
into his films, along with the music and sound effects that
accompanied his stage performances.

     If the content of Tati's dialogue is incidental, the
sound of the dialogue is not. Tati proves to be a master
of expressive sound effects. According to Cauliez, Mon Oncle is a film in which sound was treated with the same importance as visuals throughout. The film's opposing forces,
the world of the Arpels and the world of Hulot, are constantly contrasted by the use of sound. The Arpel's side of life
echoes with constant mechanical whirring, clanking, buzzing
and rattling of innumerable gadgets and appliances. When
Gérard arrives home from school one day he hears the
familiar drone of his mother's vacuum cleaner and calls for
her. No one answers. Gérard soon discovers a new automatic vacuum cleaner which is cleaning the floors while his
mother is off doing something else. Madame Arpel's household chores become a veritable cacophony of sounds. Hulot's world is quieter; the sounds that characterize the old
quarter are laughter, arguments, singing and the merry
chirping of Hulot's canary. Tati's sound effects are an integral part of his gags. The many sounds of the Arpel's
household, Hulot's squeaking window and the gurgling of the
Arpel's fish sculpture are examples of sounds used to enhance the comedy within a situation. Tati's de-emphasis of

dialogue, in addition to his reliance on visuals and sound effects has allowed him to be a truly international filmmaker.
Tati's films, neeless to say, seldom require subtitles.

It is interesting to note that Tati shot both a French
version and an English version of Mon Oncle concurrently.
Dialogue spoken in a scene was repeated a second time in
phonetically correct English after Tati had first gotten the
take he wanted in French. Consequently, minor variations
in action and camera angles can be detected between the
two versions. The English version was edited ten minutes
shorter, as well.

Frank Barcellini's and Alain Romans' music was effective in heightening the duality between the film's two
worlds. Jazz rhythms along with musique concrète (music
created by distorting various sounds that have been recorded onto magnetic tape) underscore life in the modern part
of the city. Waltzes and a theme that is essentially a
French chanson characterize Hulot's side of the film's structure, lending to it an even gentler, old-fashioned and, perhaps, more fragile quality.

After its extensive editing and sound-dubbing processes the film was released in 1958. It proved to be the most
financially successful French film of the year. Mon Oncle
won the Special Jury Prize at the Cannes Film Festival.
The following year, after its critically successful release in
the U.S., the film won the Academy Award for the Best
Foreign Film of the Year. Pierre Marcabru placed Mon
Oncle's success in the context of the day:

> In the milieu of the great misery of French cine-
> ma, more and more abandoned by laughter, more
> and more closed to humor, Jacques Tati seems a
> phenomenon. [85]

At the time, Arthur Knight said of the French film industry:

> That the present offers no new, clear-cut themes
> or trends except ... an increased absorption with
> sex, is in itself a reflection of the uncertainties
> and lack of direction within the country since the
> war. [86]

It was filmmakers with the individuality and the self-confi-
dence of René Clair, Sacha Guitry and Tati who managed to

produce valuable works in the uninspiring environment of early and mid-fifties French cinema. In this unstimulating and sobering environment at home, along with an American audience impatiently awaiting Hulot's next appearance, <u>Mon Oncle</u> stood out very obviously as a work of unique excellence.

CHAPTER 8

PLAYTIME

Hulot had, by the end of the 1950's, become such a popular film figure that Tati had been offered an American television series of 15-minute programs, which he quickly turned down: "Why should I put myself between spaghetti and Danish beer?"[87] Tati had been observing how television was changing the face of the film industry. With television so popular, films now had to offer something special. The smaller, less pretentious films could easily be lost in the scramble for the public's attention. The problem for Tati was that the required scope of production was creating "prohibitive costs for doing a film in his manner, that is more spontaneously, with many trials to get a gag right...."[88] What followed for Tati, after Mon Oncle, was the longest period of time between any two of his feature films. Tati felt that the conditions must be just right in order for him to go into production. The size of the film that Tati wanted to make and the snail's pace of production that he insisted upon required that he have everything planned to the smallest detail. The New York Times reported in early 1965 that Tati

> appears to be emerging from limbo. The latest word from Paris is that after three years of preparation the versatile writer-actor-director finally has arrived at the shooting stage of his fourth feature, which is tentatively but obviously titled 'Tati No. 4.'[89]

The film was finally to be called Playtime and would involve the largest cast, crew and sets employed to date and would be shot in 70 millimeter with stereophonic sound. Tati hired the cast and crew for an unusually lengthy one-year period, insuring himself of the time needed to bring his ideas to fruition.

76

In the new film Tati expanded the size of his representative microcosm of the world. Instead of a sleepy
French village, a tiny resort or a few Parisian neighbor-
hoods, Tati chose to stage his film in the heart of ultramodern Paris. As early as 1959, Tati had reported that his
"next film will be about people from many lands who, when
they come together, find that their troubles and needs are
much alike."[90] Tati assembled an international cast, again
mostly amateurs, very much like the assortment of people
in Les Vacances. Tati's Parisian setting easily represented
any modern city in the world. The cluster of tourists that
thread their way through the film could have been visiting
New York or Tokyo as easily as they were visiting Paris.

When Hulot was packed off to the provinces by his
brother-in-law Arpel, nearly a decade earlier, he left behind a Paris, and a world, that he could still recognize.
Even if the Arpels had built their little island of shiny new
technological bliss, Hulot still maintained his pied-à-terre
in the charming old quarter of the city. When Hulot was
next seen striding through the streets of his hometown, he
appears as a fish out of water. Few remnants are seen of
the gentle world that once was; no places of refuge are left.
Hulot "finds a capital whose celebrated monuments are only
reflections"[91] in the glass doors of the many skyscrapers.
One is very lucky to catch a glimpse of the Eiffel Tower or
the Arc de Triomphe reflected in a door as it quickly swings
open or closed. The Paris of yesterday is seen as a reflection or a dream. Tati's sentimental longing for the values and lifestyles of yesterday is, again, represented in his
satirical treatment of the commonplace.

The huge set, constructed outside Paris by a hundred
workers over the course of five months, accurately represented the cavernous, glass structured, modern Paris.
Each "skyscraper" was outfitted with swinging or "wild"
walls to allow easier camera placement and movement.
Each structure was, likewise, provided with its own central
heating system. The set, soon dubbed "Tati-ville," took on
all the markings of a real city. Two electric generators
produced enough power for a town of 15,000 people, the
streets were all paved, there was a working system of traffic signals and neon signs, all this was rounded out with
production offices, dressing rooms and dining facilities for
the cast and crew. Tati even went to the extreme of having
the buildings placed on a system of rails so that they could
be rearranged for different scenes in the film. That "Tati-

ville" became somewhat of a tourist attraction is easily understood. Visiting foreign dignitaries were taken out to
look at Tati's creation. A woman's clothing designer used
the elaborate setting as a backdrop in presenting his spring
designs. An English film producer wanted to shoot a ballet
on the set. One is reminded of the mammoth setting for
D. W. Griffith's Intolerance which, visible from all over
Los Angeles, became one of the bigger attractions of its
day. Tati had hopes of preserving the set for use by young
filmmakers. But, as if it were a scene from one of his
own films, the construction of a new highway necessitated
its being torn down.

Cauliez has described Playtime as "a supplement to
an astonishing triptych."[92] Cauliez views Tati's first three
films as elements leading to the synthesis that is Playtime.
Tati himself maintains that Playtime be considered his last
film, that it be screened last in any retrospective showings
of his films and that Trafic, his latest film to date, not be
considered the culmination of his work. By the time Playtime was released in 1967 one was able to gain some perspective on the body of Tati's work. The themes of the
earlier films stand out more clearly when compared to the
themes in Playtime. The international cast of Les Vacances
more clearly represents mankind in general, as does the
cast of Playtime. The relentless encroachment by the new
order on the older way of life seems completed in Playtime.
One can see that the gentle world of Jour de Fête and Les
Vacances was losing ground by the time Mon Oncle arrived
and was completely lost, except within the hearts of some
characters, by the time Playtime was presented. Cauliez
has described Playtime as a film that integrates many of Tati's earlier elements. The merry-go-round in Jour de Fête
is represented by the merry-go-round of cars in a traffic
jam (the circling cars slow to a halt, a little girl drops a
coin in a parking meter, the cars start moving again). The
motley crew of vacationers in Les Vacances seems nearly
identical to the excited flock of American tourists in Playtime and the chic but impractical Royal Garden restaurant
seems to echo the Arpel's lifestyle in Mon Oncle. Cauliez
feels that Playtime is more than a simple opposition of new
versus old. It goes beyond the earlier films by the "notion
of integration."[93]

If Tati's themes in Playtime were ambitious, the over-
grown technology of the Western world versus the values of
humanism, the scale of the film was just as ambitious. The

setting, described above, could easily have outdistanced the
comedy. Walter Kerr has written of what he terms "epic
comedies" that the problem was to see that the comedy was
not crushed by the scale: "Scale is normally the enemy of
humor, if only because the little man becomes difficult to
find in such mass."[94] However, Tati purposely staged his
film so that Hulot would be seen for a moment and then
lost sight of in the intricate cityscape. Tati had been steadily de-emphasizing his main character, which became apparent in this film. He had reached a level of comic observation in this film where the masses of people on the street
were playing as important a role as Hulot himself. Entire
scenes are played with only the incidental appearance of
Hulot.

In dealing with the overwhelming contemporary world,
Tati is able to find comedy and adventure within the most
mundane activities. Hulot does not contend with speeding
trains, gun fights or barroom brawls. Much of what Hulot
deals with are the commonplace events that modern life has
made so perilous. A simple walk down a crowded city
street can be a great adventure. Contending with modern
appliances or foolish modern architecture may provide man
with some of his biggest daily challenges. Hulot's simple
pursuit of Monsieur Giffard, the rather thin premise of the
film's sketchy plot, is to him an adventure. Hulot manages
to run afoul of most everything the technological world
throws in or near his path. Like the comedy heroes who
dealt with the perils of an earlier age, Hulot deals heroi-
cally with those perils peculiar to this over complicated
modern age.

Tati had painstakingly constructed his settings with
a uniformity of appearance. The opening sequence of the
film gives one the impression of sitting in the lobby of a
large and modern office building. The nearly empty room
starts to fill with people: a group of nuns, someone who
looks like a doctor, an elderly couple. The place takes on
the appearance of a hospital waiting room. As more and
more characters slowly appear, one begins to realize that
the room is a waiting room at Paris' Orly airport. What
is the difference between an office building's lobby and a
hospital waiting room as far as contemporary architecture
is concerned? Questions such as these start to form beneath the surface comedy. As one follows the film's action
throughout the city, one gets the sense of a never changing
location. Every glass and steel building looks the same.

Tati in the scaffolding of Playtime's elaborate city setting.
(Courtesy French Film Office.)

Travel posters seen on the walls of one building depict
scenes from around the world; each poster depicts the very
same building. The implication is obvious: no matter where
one travels, even romantic Paris, everything looks alike.
The blandness of the modern world has reduced everything
to the same level: the lowest common denominator. Tati
has been quoted as saying:

> I wanted this uniformity; all the chairs, for in-
> stance, in the restaurant, in the bank--they're all
> the same. The floor's the same, the paint's the
> same. It costs a lot of money, of course, but it's
> there and it's not more expensive than Sophia Lor-
> en.[95]

The location's drabness was heightened by using large photo blowups to replace background glass walls in order to reduce the number of reflections. Tati felt the reflections were too attractive.

The universe created within Tati's films is an eccentric one. It may take an ininitiated audience a few moments to settle in with the pacing, the exploration of details and the gags that can suddenly spring from any character or direction. R. C. Dale has described the mood of Playtime's oddly staged opening scene:

> Playtime opens with a long shot--long both in terms of its duration as a take and in its camera position--of a mammoth reception hall peopled by only a middle-aged couple speaking in hushed whispers.... Their whispers and the extraordinarily antiseptic qualities of the vast hall suggest that we are in the lobby of a huge, brand new hospital. After a considerable while another figure peeks out from behind a partition, looks around slowly and gradually emerges to mop the floor in that erratic, jumpy mannerism that Tati somehow manages to convey to his actors. Eventually, after Tati has made it perfectly clear that this is his movie and that he's running it his own way, on his own terms, and that it's important that we retain the opening shot, he begins the proper action. [96]

Tati is here analyzing or, more accurately, dissecting the scene in such a way that one is able to view the commonplace anew, with all the attendant comedy. It becomes more than just a waiting room full of people. It is not uncommon for Tati to create a moment of confusion or mystery at the beginning of a scene such as this. He will then reveal, either in a flash or step by step, such as here, what the scene really depicts. By having one's established point of view disoriented momentarily, one can see a familiar scene with a new objectivity.

Tati is operating in Playtime beyond (or beneath the surface of) the story and comedy situations. Tati treats us here to a veritable ballet of movements by the masses of characters. The movements of the characters are effectively orchestrated in such a way that the film's overall dramatic progression is mirrored in the way the characters move. The opening of the film has been described as "oppressively

Hulot ascends the escalator for a bird's-eye view of the office maze below him.   Cardboard cut-outs serve as figures
in the far background.   Playtime (1967).   (Courtesy Columbia Pictures.)

---

linear."97   The characters in the airport lobby walk in
straight lines.   Barbara, the young American tourist playing
essentially the same role as Martine in Les Vacances, is
seen shuffling through a housewares display in a large department store.   She is accompanied by her group of fellow
women tourists.   Barbara turns her eyes away from the
architecture's linear dictates for a fleeting moment in order
to catch sight of Hulot involved in some gag.   Early in the
film Hulot is lost in a maze of tiny office cubicles as he
searches for Monsieur Giffard, a man with whom he has a
business appointment.   Filmed from above in a characteristic wide angle, one observes Hulot like a rat scurrying
about a gigantic maze.   Even when Giffard is visible to the
audience he is unseen by Hulot.   The harshly linear struc-

ture of the office building is clearly ridiculous when seen
from the point of view Tati allows his audience to take.
Jonathan Rosenbaum has observed from the film:

> Pursuing the action in straight lines, we become
> victimized, imprisoned by the architecture, much
> in the way that Giffard, rushing directly towards
> one of the characters resembling Hulot (the film
> has several) in an early sequence, runs smack in-
> to a glass door. An alternate method of looking
> is Tati's message'. [98]

Tati has described the use of character's movement within
the film:

> It's a little like a ballet. At the beginning, the
> people's movements always follow the architecture,
> they never make a curve, they go from one line
> to another. The more the picture continues, the
> more the people dance, and start to make curves,
> and turn around, and start to be absolutely round--
> because we have decided that we're still there. [99]

When the characters reach the newly built Royal Garden
nightclub, in one of the film's last sequences, their movement dissolves into swirls, loops and circles, totally dis-
solving the straight lines that were impressed upon them
earlier. Rosenbaum describes how the audience, as well,
must loosen its own pattern of watching the action:

> It is virtually essential that we curve the trajec-
> tory of our gaze: if our eyes attempt to traverse
> the screen in straight lines, we simply miss too
> much. [100]

Tati had steadily been giving room to more and more
characters in his films. Although François dominated Tati's
first feature, Hulot began sharing the spotlight with others
as early as the film in which he first appeared. By the
time he had made Playtime, Tati very nearly reduced Hulot
to just one of the many characters. Hulot, invented by Tati as a character who embodies those qualities common to
all men, was effectively blending in with his surroundings.
Tati was reaching the "democratic comedy" he had thought
about for so long. Roy Armes has described Hulot in Playtime as an "episodic chapter." [101] As much screen time is
spent following the gang of tourists as is spent following Hu-

lot. Tati even, interestingly, introduces another "Hulot";
a man dressed exactly like Hulot, down to the long stemmed
pipe clenched in his teeth, is seen working his way through
the housewares show early in the film. It is as if Tati is
giving a hint of what is to follow. Tati gives the audience
the opportunity to construct its own film; to follow whichever characters it chooses; to decide just who the film's
star should be. The comedy of life is found among the people on the street. It is necessary for one to view life se-
lectively and with such a point of view that life's inherent
comedy is revealed. Jean L'Hote has written of the unseen
Hulot:

> Ideally, Tati would like a film of the adventures
> of Hulot in which Hulot himself does not appear.
> His presence would be apparent simply from the
> more or less catastrophic upheavals left in his
> wake. How many directors have a comparable
> respect for their public or such confidence in
> their public's imagination?[102]

Tati's intuition has shown him that it is often funnier
watching an average person doing a stunt than to watch the
antics of a character who announces by his appearance that
he will be amusing. In _Playtime_ Tati has taken his biggest
step toward showing the humor in ordinary people. Tati's
stated intention toward his audience has been "to prove to
them that, in spite of everything, every week or month
something happens to them and that the comic effect belongs
to everyone."[103]

In de-emphasizing Hulot, Tati allowed the settings to
play a bigger and bigger part. Locations have always fascinated Tati. The village in _Jour de Fête_, the little hotel
in _Les Vacances_ and the fascinatingly different homes in
Mon Oncle play as large a part in their films as any characters. In lessening the importance of Hulot, Tati still
maintains the importance of the effect Hulot has on things.
Hulot may only pass through a scene very quickly, but he
may leave behind a trail of things he has upset. In the
shiny steel and glass world of _Playtime_, Tati goes so far
as to reduce Hulot to a mere reflection in one scene. Giffard eagerly pursues Hulot through the maze of the office
building until he finally catches sight of him. Giffard rush-
es forward to greet Hulot, not realizing that he is actually
approaching Hulot's reflection in a window. When Giffard
steps outside he is startled to see that Hulot has disappeared.

Of Tati's working with amateurs, Cauliez has observed: "He chooses people for their nature, not for their talent."[104] Tati cast his own film distributor as the man demonstrating the inflatable chairs in the housewares show. An electronics expert portrays the man who demonstrates the push brooms mounted with headlights. Tati was able to herd up the entire bunch of American lady tourists by attending an armed forces luncheon in the guise of a waiter. Even the film's assistant director was used to portray a chauffeur. Barbara Dennek, who plays the typically Tati-esque female lead, was a mother's helper down the street from Tati's home. Tati simply wants his players to represent themselves, doing no more than they normally would. Mary Blume observed the simplicity that Tati asks of his cast:

> The actors need only walk past each other, but the choreography needs perfect timing and someone is always off. 'The French are a bit too slow,' Tati says after filming ends, 'Americans know more how to move. The French are verbal.'[105]

With the decreased appearances of Hulot, Tati was doing what all good teachers do. He was requiring his audience to expand their abilities at observation and to look for new things. If the audience went into the theater expecting to watch Hulot for two hours they could have easily been disappointed. If they were able to construct their own comedy from the lively tableau spread before them, then they were able to be entertained. Blume pointed out:

> The problem with Playtime is that people wait for what is not in the picture. The moment they wait for what is not, they miss what is.... One of the things they waited for was Mr. Hulot whose appearances were just episodic. The humor of the film lies in its details, not in its characters.[106]

The harsh and unyielding city seems to be accepted by both the excited tourists and its inhabitants. The tourists cheerfully make the most of their vacation spot and the inhabitants seem either unaware of or thoroughly conditioned to the rigors of their city. There is a submissive quality to the characters in the film. James Monaco wrote:

> The genius of Playtime is just in the totally sub-
> missive character of its people.... By extrapo-
> lating that mindless submission to a cast of hun-
> dreds, Tati has been able to achieve the kind of
> power and sense that Ionesco always just missed.[107]

However, Monaco goes on to describe the characters in the
film as possessing an "indomitable spirit." As washed
along by circumstance as Hulot can be, his very eccentricity is an indication that his spirit resists surrender. And
Hulot is merely a representative of the mass of people in
the film. Beneath the surface docility there is a great enthusiasm for life buried inside everyone. As the regimentation of Playtime crumbles away, the spirit of people
bursts forth in the wild spontaneity of the nightclub sequence.

Tati is not, however, the documentarian of day-to-
day life that one might think. He can not resist fiddling
with the settings and objects before him. He composes
reality in such a way that one is able to see the similari-
ties between seemingly different actions and objects. Tati
views the world metaphorically. An office becomes a maze,
a crowded traffic circle becomes a slowly revolving merry-
go-round of cars, collapsing nightclub decorations form a
fence and streetlamps appear to be clusters of flowers.
Stanley Kauffmann found fault with Tati's meddling with the
universe:

> Tati can not rest with observation, he has to ar-
> range. A minister in a drugstore pauses in front
> of a neon sign 'Drugstore' as the 'o' lights up,
> giving him a halo.... From sharp comment we
> decline through pointless points to cuteness.[108]

Penelope Gilliatt described Tati's story outline for
Playtime as "probably the smallest script ever to be made
in 70mm."[109] The plot takes second place to the film's
gags and, given the technical scope of the film, is amazingly simple. A group of chattering American women de-
bark at Orly airport. The film follows them on their tour
as they vainly attempt to catch a glimpse of the Paris they
have heard so much about. Hulot, in vain as well, tries
to find Monsieur Giffard with whom he has a business appointment, most likely an interview for a job. Slowly but
inevitably Hulot's path starts to cross that of the women until the two paths become entangled at the film's end. Bar-

bara, a pretty young lady who is uncharacteristically quiet
amongst her garrulous companions, catches sight of the eccentrically amusing Hulot and establishes a nonverbal rap-
port with him. The tourists culminate their day in Paris
with a wild party at the newly opened Royal Garden nightclub and head back to Orly airport early the next morning.
Barbara carries with her a small bouquet and scarf given
her by the shyly gallant Hulot in a moment of bravery.
Ironically, depicted upon the scarf are views of the real
Paris, the Paris she never got to see.

   Kauffmann insists that Tati's film be founded upon
the principles of sound dramatic structure, with each scene
a stepping stone toward a final resolution of a conflict. He
found little point or need in many of Playtime's comedy sequences:

> Hulot goes to see someone in an immense office
> building and waits downstairs after being an-
> nounced, sitting on a sofa. The man he has asked
> for appears at the far end of a long corridor, the
> sound of his heels approaching. Two or three
> times as we watch the man trudging along toward
> us, Hulot rises and the hallman gestures for him
> to remain seated, there's plenty of time. The
> moment takes its point of contrast with human-
> size buildings. But the whole sequence comes to
> nothing. 110

Tati's intention in such a sequence is to examine a certain
behavior and a certain style of architecture. Both Hulot's
action in standing to greet the approaching Giffard and the
apparent size of the building are looked at with objectivity.
The point of the scene is to realize the ridiculousness inherent in such everyday activities. A Tati work is essentially a filmic exploration of a location or a process and
not necessarily a dramatic struggle.

   Tati does not entirely assume authorship of his films.
If Tati's subject matter is chosen freely, without regimentation, there is also a freedom in the way in which it is
presented. Tati paints a huge canvas, much like a painting
by Brueghel, depicting a myriad of activities, and allows
the audience to select where it will direct its attention.
Rosenbaum noted:

> Comedy has conventionally meant everybody laugh-
> ing at the same things at the same time; whereas
> in Playtime, for an audience really to respond to
> it, different people have to laugh at different
> things at different times. [111]

Tati is aware of how easily people's tastes are regimented.
He has expressed concern that the conventional way of structuring comedies may be considered the only acceptable approach: "If we accept ... a comic picture to be constructed
a certain way because that's the way people will laugh ...
we're going to be part of a regiment."[112] The use of wide
screen 70mm with Tati's predilection for the wide angle
shot overcomes this regimentation. The audience is left to
its own perceptions, selecting that which interests them
most. Rosenbaum observed that the background within any
scene is actually that which the audience chooses to ignore.
As Cauliez said, "Why reserve the big screen just for cav-
alry charges?"[113] Tati has commented that

> The images are designed so that after you see the
> picture two or three times, it's no longer my
> film, it starts to be your film. You recognize
> the people, you know them and you don't even
> know who directed the picture. It's not a film
> you sign like Fellini: Roma. Playtime is no-
> body. [114]

Sequences of gags evolving out of a given location
are the building blocks of Tati's films. When one remembers Playtime, the sequence that stands as the central pil-
lar of the film's construction is the scene in the Royal Garden nightclub. This sequence could, indeed, stand on its
own as a separate film entitled, perhaps, The Destruction
of the Nightclub. Looking at Playtime's structure dramatically, the Royal Garden scene would stand at the film's
climax. It is the point at which all the film's characters
are brought together and is, also, the point at which humanity is seen triumphing over the dictates of technology and
design. The Royal Garden is a brand new nightclub that is
not quite ready for its opening night. Floor tiles have just
been laid, decorations hastily installed and nothing, as yet,
has even been tried out when the wandering band of tourists
descends upon the unwary establishment. What follows is
an intricately staged, step by step, dissolution of the nightclub. As the Royal Garden starts to go to pieces, the customers enjoy themselves, dancing more and more boister-

ously among the raining debris.   The jazz band swings from
cool to hot jazz as the activity intensifies.   Tati uses his
wide-angle lens here to great advantage.   He builds one gag
on top of the next until the entire room is filled with activity.   As every little thing in the room starts to misfunc-
tion one must zero in on specific activities, following whatever interests one the most.   Rather than a humorous analysis of one thing at a time, Tati chooses here to hit the
audience with almost everything at once.   The impact is
startling.   As in the films of Renoir or Buñuel, where a
violent shock is often delivered to the film's group of complacent bourgeois, Tati administers the shock of disorderliness and confusion to his complacent group.   His characters respond joyously as if Tati had tapped their hidden
spirit and spontaneity.   As the chic nightclub crumbles
around the ears of the merrymakers, Tati has brought them
from the numbing regimentation of the film's early scenes
to its opposite: humanity expressed through chaos.   The ro-
bot-like movements and perceptions of the characters gradually slide into anarchy over the course of the film until
circular, swirling, drunken spontaneity is reached.   The
humanity expressed by Hulot in Les Vacances and by Hulot
and Gérard in Mon Oncle is expressed by the entire group
in Playtime.   Hulot need not stand alone.

   The nightclub scene takes up about a third of the
film's length.   The importance of the scene to the entire
picture has been expressed in Tati's description:

> I had to work out each part and direct each char-
> acter separately.   It took me seven weeks to
> shoot it.   First I'd set up all the different move-
> ments in the background, then I'd set up each ac-
> tion in the foreground, looking through the lens
> while composing each shot so I could see every-
> thing at once.   I had to shoot it all in sequence;
> there was no other way. [115]

   Tati's gags are of their usual originality, but he
compounds more gags into one space and one time than
ever before.   The first step in the eventual destruction of
the nightclub comes when the tiles on the dance floor stick
to the feet of the maitre d'.   A platter of fish is too long
to pass through the opening from the kitchen to the dining
room.   As the fish is placed on a cart and wheeled to its
table, one watches as one eager waiter after another walks
by and seasons the fish to his liking.   Tati does not linger

to watch the customer's reaction to the over-seasoned dish.
He moves on to the next bit of business. The amiable doorman swings the glass front door open and shut for each of
the club's arriving customers. The door eventually shatters
into tiny pieces, but the doorman unflinchingly retains his
grip on the door handle. He continues to swing the handle,
with its imaginary door still attached, back and forth as
people pass in and out of the doorway. He will even follow
people across the lobby, opening and closing the "door" for
them as they go. The gag is funny as well as being double
edged. What is the purpose of an all-glass door? Does the
doorman not serve one as well by opening and closing the
make-believe door? These questions come to mind behind
the humor and give one a chance to look at some conventions with a new perspective. The wrought iron backs of
the nightclub's chairs are designed so poorly that their imprint is left on the back of anyone sitting on them. When
some "artistic" ceiling decorations start to fall and are left
hanging by their wires, the rowdy American businessman
employs them as a fence. He rounds up all the people with
imprints on their backs and allows them into the private
party he stages behind the makeshift fence. It is important
to note that Hulot is not excluded from this exclusive group.
One should compare this Hulot with the lonely Hulot in the
masquerade party scene from Les Vacances. Although still
eccentric, he is much less the outsider than he used to be.

     Tati has always believed that it is funnier to see a
dignified person do something funny than to watch someone
funny do the same action. The sudden incongruity between
someone's high notion of himself and the embarrassing realities of life is always amusing. The Royal Garden sequence is a projection of this idea onto a bigger plane. The
nightclub itself is the essence of slick "chic-dom." The
very name, Royal Garden, is an example of pomposity.
When the nightclub starts to fall to pieces, it is the same
as watching a pompously smug person slip on a banana peel.

     The Royal Garden sequence can also be seen as a
continuation of the themes in earlier Tati films. The second-rate Hôtel de la Plage from Les Vacances becomes
the first-class Royal Garden. The unsuccessful masquerade
party, with Hulot as the only participant, becomes the wildly crowded nightclub scene. One also recalls Hulot attempting vainly to fit in at the Arpel's stylish cocktail party in
Mon Oncle. As the style of the Royal Garden falls to pieces
it becomes easier and easier for Hulot to fit in there. The

international mixture of guests in the Hôtel de la Plage directly parallels the group of people that converge upon the
sorry nightclub, as well.

Even though Tati's use of the camera is straightforward and quite basic, his use of sound is, to say the least,
innovative. With Playtime's 70-millimeter image size, the
width of which allowed room for more soundtracks on the
film, five-track, magnetic, stereophonic sound became possible. Tati is one of the few filmmakers who makes known
his interest in the improved sound quality of magnetic soundtracks over the more conventional optical tracks. One of
the factors that held up the U.S. release of Playtime was
Tati's hope that it would only be released in the 70-millime-
ter format for the sake of sound quality as well as visual
quality. The five tracks of sound on the 70-millimeter version of Playtime allow for increased subtleties and richness;
something that was sacrificed when Tati found it necessary
to release it in 35 as well as 70 millimeter. The quality of
sound is crucial to Tati who considers the building of his
soundtracks to be, essentially, a reshooting of the film.
Tati claims to film most of the scenes in his films without
sound and claims to add the few voices and the variety of
sound effects while in the controlled atmosphere of the studio.

Sound effects are used for expressive as well as humorous purposes in Tati's films. The buzzing of the neon
signs throughout Playtime lend an eerie and almost surreal-
istic quality. Sitting in the waiting room of the large office
building, Hulot notices that the cushions of the chairs slowly
pop back into shape after the person sitting on them has
risen. Simply observing Hulot's reaction to the movements
of the cushion is funny. When Tati adds the expressive
sound of a pneumatic "wooshing" the scene grows even funnier. As before, the human voice plays as important a part
in the scheme of Tati's soundtracks as any other sound effect. With the film's mixture of nationalities one is treated
to a cacophony of bits of various languages. Cauliez labeled
Playtime as the first film made in the language of "Fran-
glais." James Monaco has described the use of voices as
"a language which is a kind of sonorous backdrop to the important part of the soundtrack...."[116] Stanley Kauffmann
again seems to be the one voice of disagreement. He considers Tati's soundtracks to be indistinct and unexpressive,
with one element working against the next: "Once again, the
soundtrack is a designed burble, rather than clear dialogue
or clear silence."[117]

Francis Lemarque's musical themes are in constant juxtaposition to the harsher, jazzier themes of David Stein and James Campbell. Eventually, Lemarque's chansons win out over the competition just as the hidden spirit of the film's characters is finally victorious. Cauliez observed a clear musical structure within the Royal Garden sequence, from a walkurie to a more human cancan.[118] The softer strains of music that accompany the film's gentle denouement represent a humanity that will always prevail over the demands of any age.

R. C. Dale has gone so far as to describe the structure of the overall film as that of a musical fugue with Hulot and Barbara as separate elements that are wound closer and closer together as their paths cross and recross. Dale observes Tati's purpose to be an establishment of the fact that human contact is still possible "despite the horrific labyrinth"[119] of the modern city. He sees the film as starting on a long chord: the airport waiting room, people sitting alone quietly. With the introduction of Barbara and of Hulot one is presented the two themes of the film: the visitor come to the city and the old man lost in the new city. These simple themes are built upon, pushing Hulot and Barbara together and then apart. The tempo is increased throughout, until both a visual and musical climax is reached when Hulot finally meets Barbara formally, in the Royal Garden sequence.

Barbara, playing a similar role to that of Martine in Les Vacances, serves to soften the comedy by allowing Hulot to reveal a bit more of his romantic side. Barbara also serves as a connecting element between Hulot and the rest of the characters, although this is much less needed than in earlier films. Barbara offers a few, much needed moments of sanity. Hulot represents the standards and manners of the Old World, of a time gone by, and Barbara allows him to express his gentlemanly manner. Together they demonstrate that there are still reasons for the old values.

As the bus winds its way back along the highway toward the airport, Barbara examines the small bouquet; she looks up to notice the row of streetlamps whizzing past. The flowers and streetlamps have the identical shape. Tati has said of this: "If one person who sees lampposts along the road is able to smile in remembering Playtime, then I have won."[120] Tati clearly sees the small moments of gen-

tility or romance as victories over the technological world.
A bouquet of flowers, a gentle piece of music, a genuine
smile are all proof that one has not surrendered one's own
humanity. Tati has summed up Playtime and, perhaps, his
outlook on life in general, in this simple statement: "If one
can not humanize the world, at least one can make poetry
of the city."121

As discussed earlier, Tati's story structure is such
that he does not end his films with any great resolutions,
but rather ends them quietly. In the case of Playtime, Tati finds it necessary to have the curtains drawn in the theater as soon as he dissolves from the flowers in Barbara's
hand to the streetlamps.

Playtime was completed with Tati's own money. He
has made a habit of pouring the profits from one film into
the production of the next. The cost of finishing the film
was unusually high, well above anything Tati had spent before. Tati found it necessary to mortgage his home in
Saint-Germain. Although he was technically flat broke, he
had completed what many critics consider to be his master-
piece. Jonathan Rosenbaum wrote:

> It is regrettable ... that Bazin didn't live to see
> Tati's masterpiece. To some degree, Playtime
> can be regarded as an embodiment and extension
> of Bazin's most cherished ideas about deep-focus,
> long takes, and the 'democratic' freedoms that
> these techniques offer to the spectator.122

Naturally, there were the usual difficulties with distributors who wanted to bill the film in the United States as
Mr. Hulot in Playtime. Tati refused; it was a film about
everybody, not simply Hulot. So much money was involved
in the film that concern about public acceptance was unusually high. The distributors were able to convince Tati to
shorten the film by fifteen minutes after its Paris premiere.
Tati has commented on this: "Of course it didn't help any.
You either accept it or you don't."123 The English version
of the film was subsequently cut sizably from two hours and
thirty minutes to two hours. The versions seen most often
in America may or may not contain a scene where Hulot
stands in the street at night, looking in through the huge
wall-sized picture windows of two adjacent apartments, one
of them Giffard's, and watches each family settle in for an
evening at home. Tati has since stated that the original
version of the film is the only one he believes in.

Playtime was released in France only to those theaters equipped with 70-millimeter stereophonic facilities.
Tati did not provide a 35-millimeter version for the lower-
priced theaters. Consequently, the film was commercially
unsuccessful in France. The lack of enthusiasm for the
film in its homeland made it an unlikely prospect for expor-
tation to the U.S. Rosenbaum observed just a few years
ago:

> It can be argued, of course, that Tati has offered
> his audience too much freedom, and over-estimat-
> ed the capacities of several spectators--one rea-
> son, perhaps, why five years after its Paris open-
> ing, Playtime has yet to receive an American re-
> lease.[124]

The film was not released in the United States until the middle of 1973, half a year after the later Trafic was released.
If the distributors were concerned about the film's chances
for a commercial success, Tati was concerned that the film
be released in only its 70-millimeter stereo format. Tati
had held out until it became obvious that American distributors would not even consider the film with such a set of restrictions on it. Ironically, the distributors' commercial
considerations coincided with Tati's artistic considerations
in one respect: American audiences saw the films in the order Tati, himself, would choose to present them, Trafic
first and then Playtime.

Although financial difficulties followed for Tati, he
had accomplished what he had set out to do. He has stated:

> I'm proud of Playtime, it's exactly the picture I
> wanted to make.... I've suffered a lot because of
> it, physically and financially, but it's really the
> film I wanted to do.[125]

R. C. Dale has recalled that he first went to see the
film "expecting to be mildly amused" and came away "bursting with admiration and enthusiasm."[126] It is interesting to
consider the ferocity of Tati's independence. Like any filmmaker who must contend with as large a budget as Playtime's
and, at the same time, refuse to make concessions to commercial pressure, Tati must have stubbornly held his artistic ground while making great personal sacrifices.

Playtime's humorously satiric analysis of the contemporary set of styles and values (architecture, manners, concepts of beauty and the many other ways people express themselves) can be seen in many lights. To most people Playtime is an entertaining and eccentric comedy whose impact is delivered in an unexpected manner. It is satire played at a farcical level; it can also stand as an omen for the future. Although the characters and settings in the film may seem a bit ridiculous, they are not so very much exaggerated from reality. Even every joke made has its base in this humdrum reality. The mindless obedience with which most of the characters approach the conditions of life is not so different from the obedience one can be witness to in the real world. Tati is showing people what they have already started to become although may not yet be aware of. Tati observed a few years after the completion of Playtime that the film's comedy may not have been as frivolous as it seemed. He spoke of a new highway that was planned for construction alongside Notre Dame cathedral:

> In thirty or forty-five years they'll find it [building the highway] was so wrong, because it [Notre Dame] was so well built and arranged now. Boys play guitars there and the girls go and have little love affairs with them. That's Paris. That's why I did Playtime. [127]

CHAPTER 9

TRAFIC

Tati's fifth feature film holds an odd place in the overall body of his work. Trafic seems almost incidental to, or out of place with, the path Tati's films had been taking. The culmination of both themes and size of production in Playtime appears to mark the last step in the logical progression or expansion of Tati's films. One must have asked, after Playtime, where Tati could go from there. In both Mon Oncle and especially Playtime Tati had made effective and universal observations on the changing values of the world. Yet, there still remained vulnerable areas of modern life that cried out for Tati's touch. Tati chose to look at the one invention that had dictated the pattern of modern life more than any other: the automobile. Tati recognized that the degree to which humans identify with their cars and allow their cars to dominate them was good material for farce and satire.

In surveying Tati's films, one gets a sense that Trafic is out of place. It would have fit in more logically between Mon Oncle and Playtime, with Tati satirizing modern homes and life styles in one, the conventions of transportation and travel in the next, and culminating in an analysis of the city, representing the contemporary world in general. Tati himself has commented:

> I always show Playtime after Trafic. On the basis of my intentions, Trafic could have been shot before Playtime. Playtime will always be my last picture because of the dimension of the decor, regarding the people. 128

Trafic, a Franco-Dutch production which began filming in Holland late in 1969, is quite simply the story of Hulot, an automobile advertising artist, and his crew of assis-

96

tants who are attempting to transport the new Altra camping
car to its first public display at the Amsterdam auto show.
The story line, typically sparse, allows for innumerable
gags as Hulot races to meet the show's deadline.

James Monaco has placed Trafic in an interesting
context:

> Without the clear revelations of Playtime, Traffic
> can not be seen in proper context. The two form
> a diptych, a transcendent farce which summons
> up the twentieth-century experience in a manner
> that reminds one of no one so much as Jean-Luc
> Godard (if it can be believed)--a Godard who is
> classic rather than romantic, controlled rather
> than passionate, ironic rather than committed.
> Playtime is Tati's Deux ou Trois Choses Que Je
> Sais d'Elle and Alphaville, Traffic is Tati's Week-
> end. 129

In comparing Godard's humor in Weekend with Tati's humor
in Trafic, one sees that Godard regards the creatures who
zoom about in their cars as pitiful and stupid. Disliking
them and feeling superior, one is forced to laugh at Godard's
characters. The subjects in Tati's Trafic are as dumbly
attached to their cars as are Godard's characters, but one
feels a kinship with them. One does not look down upon the
silly behavior of Tati's people. One is allowed the space
to see one's own life within these very characters.

The title sequence of Trafic represents the themes
for the film to follow. One's ears are assaulted by the mechanical cacophony of an auto assembly plant. Car doors
are noisily stamped out of sheet metal and sent rolling down
a conveyor belt. The sequence continues until one bent and
wrinkled car door comes along the line. The laugh is a
small one; the implications are great. One immediately re-
cognizes Tati's ironic sense of the imperfect world. Not
even the sleek and smooth technology, into which one places
one's life, is free of errors.

Early in the film, Tati introduces the site of the Amsterdam auto show in a typically wide-angle, bird's-eye view
of the convention hall. Clusters of officials, spread across
the wide expanse of floor, busily stretch out pieces of string
to serve as demarcations for each auto display area. From
this distant point of view the strings themselves become in-

visible. Tati stages an incredibly ingenious ballet as each
man, moving about the hall, high steps over the invisible
string. One is gazing down upon what appears to be a flock
of long legged flamingoes sloshing about in some lagoon.
This is another example of Tati's use of the technique first
popularized by Chaplin: transposition.

Hulot is first introduced as he quietly sneaks into
his office in a Paris garage. Who knows why he sneaks to
work? Who can fathom everything that goes on inside his
head? The garage is crowded with workers who hastily assemble the Altra camping car display for the upcoming auto
show. Hulot, the company's advertising artist, is to accompany Marcel, a comically dog-faced truck driver, and Maria, an aggressive public relations woman, to the Amsterdam
show. Marcel and Hulot, in the truck carrying the camping
car, follow Maria who wrecklessly blazes the way in her tiny
sports car. The obstacles or "roadblocks" that befall them
along the way make up the body of the film.

One is eventually forced to ask oneself if Tati sees
Hulot as a different character from the ineffectual and idle
man of earlier films. Here, Hulot is, of all things, employed. He is actually seen at work, obviously more successful than at Arpel's plastics factory. Has Tati sold Hulot down the river for the price of respectability? Like the
thoroughly humanistic Hulot of Mon Oncle, the Hulot of Trafic is, however, unable to hold his job. Arriving in Amsterdam with the car on the day the show has closed, Hulot
is fired and given train fare home by his angry boss. The
audience can breathe a sigh of relief. Hulot has not sold
out. There is, however, a perceptible shift in his personality. The easily intimidated Hulot of earlier films seems
more at ease with people. Although tending towards Chaplin's independence, Hulot still retains a generous amount of
Langdon's diffidence. It is comforting to see Hulot display
more confidence and comforting to see that people accept
him despite his eccentricities.

Tati's establishment of Hulot as an employee of a
company that makes camping vehicles is not only convenient,
but well thought out. Hulot, the eternal man of nature, pro-

Opposite, top: Hulot narrowly missing disaster by the simple timing of his movements; bottom: Hulot attempting to
disentangle one of the many traffic jams. Trafic (1971).
(Both courtesy Columbia Pictures.)

Hulot and the brash public relations woman Maria (Maria
Kimberly). Trafic (1971). (Courtesy Columbia Pictures.)

moting a product that is, in essence, antithetical to nature
is ironical and symptomatic of society's convoluted values.
The little green Altra is a machine designed to bring all the
comfort and convenience of man's technology into the simple
peacefulness of the wilderness. It does not so much promote the values of nature as demean them. The vehicle is
the kind of object in which Tati saw great comic potential.
The number of convenient gadgets built inconspicuously into
the machine is unfathomable. A weekend camping with this
car would be hardly any different from a weekend at home.
The car's display for the auto show is, of course, made up
of ersatz cardboard trees and the tape recorded sounds of
birds.

     If much of the production value of Playtime was dis-
played in the elaborate construction of "Tati-ville," then
much of the value displayed in the smaller-budgeted Trafic is
seen in the cleverly built car. Tati elaborately displays his
creation when the small convoy is pulled over by Dutch police. The police lead Hulot and companions to their garage

and watch wide-eyed as the vehicle's many features are eagerly demonstrated for them. Hulot slides an awning out
the back of the car. When poles are extended to the ground
and the awning is rolled down, it becomes a tent. Each
half of the rear bumper swings out to form chairs that accompany a dining table which slides out from under the
car's floor. The two tail lights are detachable, one as a
flashlight and one as a shower nozzle. Maria, who is ha-
ranguing the police to let them go, takes time to proudly
demonstrate the sleeping accommodations. Sitting beside a
chubby policeman, Maria yanks a cord which both inflates a
bed beneath them and stretches out the car like a telescope
to allow room to lie down. She swings out a portable television and the two of them sit watching like two astronauts
in their Altra space capsule; on the screen is an Apollo
space mission. Television coverage of the Apollo 11 mission is for Tati an ironical comment on Hulot's and everyone else's earthbound problems with technology.

Hulot, seeming now to be less at odds with the
world, does not so much resist the world of the automobile
as go along obediently with its crazy demands. One is
treated here to more of an assortment of comic insights on
a certain subject than to a slapstick battle of Hulot versus
the world in general. Tati treats his material with only a
slightly more exaggerated eye than a good documentary
filmmaker. For the first time in Tati's work, he actually
includes a number of documentary sequences shot surrepti-
tiously in traffic jams and in an actual auto show. In fact
Roy Armes has observed Tati's penchant for realism to be
a strong thread running through all his films:

> Tati has constantly pursued the ideal of a realis-
> tic form of comedy. This sounds paradoxical--
> comedy would seem to imply excess and exaggera-
> tion--but Tati has followed this course throughout
> his career and his films can only be understood
> in this light. [130]

Tati's concern for basing his films in reality is re-
lated directly to his documentarian's eye. One quickly recalls the accurately depicted villages in both Jour de Fête
and Les Vacances and the painstaking reality of "Tati-ville."
The large auto exposition becomes just such a subject in
Trafic. Tati intercuts real documentary footage with staged
footage. While Tati's staged footage may look staged, the
quality of humor in the real footage blends in easily with

Tati's own constructed comedy. Many of the comical-looking
car buffs who in real life were shuffling through displays of
sleek new autos support Tati's theory that comedy abounds in
reality. The reality is not only humorous but a bit pathetic.
One begins to realize that none of these ordinary people lead
lives that can have anything at all to do with these expensive
automobiles. One gets a peculiar sense of watching children
become enamored of an object they could never own nor find
any use for. The use of documentary footage in these scenes
lends a poignancy that goes beyond surface comedy.

In a scene that was filmed and cut into the movie after its first premiere, one is treated to another elaborately
drawn setting. Hulot's entourage pulls into a gas station
that gives away lifesize plaster busts of historical figures
with each purchase of gasoline. A timid little man is handed an oversized bust of some Spanish Conquistador. The
man stares at it blankly and hands it to his wife. Another
man is handed a bust that looks exactly like himself; he does
not react in the slightest. Tati has taken a bit of realism,
the giving of gifts with the purchase of certain products, and
pushed it a tiny step further. The gifts that are handed out
are much more obviously useless than the gifts one is ac-
customed to receiving in such a situation. The scene works
because the comedy is kept close to a common reality. A-
gain, one gets the opportunity to see oneself through new
eyes.

This feeling of reality and attention to location is one
of the factors that accounts for the film's rather thin characterizations. The film is peopled with amateurs, as one expects from Tati. While this may work to advantage in the
numerous smaller roles, it fails in the lead role of Maria,
the P.R. woman. Casting an American fashion model, Maria Kimberly, as the female lead was simply Tati's inclination to cast type over talent. Unlike the earlier films, Trafic requires that the female lead be more aggressive and
display a stronger personality. Unfortunately, Maria's mis-
directed energy can even, at times overpower Hulot. The
performance is perhaps the most bothersome in any of Tati's
films. In requiring such a broadly drawn character it seems
that Tati overstepped his abilities and judgment. He ought
to allow his players essentially to play themselves and not
reach too far for a character.

At points, Tati has pushed his comedy even beyond
his own usual limits. Occasionally, he will slip from sight

gags and slapstick into an almost absurdist style. The odd
and taciturn distraction of the hotel keepers in Les Vacances
is an early example. In Trafic, after Hulot's truck runs out
of gas, he is sent walking along the endless highway, carrying a gas can in his hand. From the opposite direction
comes a young man, also carrying an empty gas can. The
two men stop and stare at each other from opposite sides of
the highway. The young man suddenly bolts and races
across a dirt field towards a nearby village. Hulot gives
pursuit. When the young man stops short and looks back
towards Hulot, Hulot quickly changes his direction, pretending he is not following the man, and starts scanning the horizon for his own gas station. When the young man again
turns and dashes off towards the village, Hulot quickly re-
sumes the chase. The two men never acknowledge one another, never speak, not even as they wait for gas beside the
same pump. The scene is madly funny. One must ask oneself why it is necessary to run off wildly in pursuit of gasoline and why Hulot pretends he is not following the young
man. A simple problem escalates into an amusingly odd
situation.

Tati's films abound with characters who, while not
necessarily bordering on the insane, are defined solely by
their peculiar little ticks and gestures. Early in the film a
young photographer gesticulates excitedly with his hands as
he speaks. Maria is constantly ordering people about in nonstop, exasperated tones. She is hardly ever still, appearing
in each new scene wearing a stunning outfit into which she
has just speedily changed. A happy-go-lucky auto repairman
nonchalantly kicks and tosses around anything from his garage that gets in his way. An elderly employee of the car
company is seen patiently carrying a sports coat on a hanger
each time he appears. This becomes the man's trademark
as surely as the quirks of other characters become theirs.

If the architecture in Playtime can be seen as taking
on the importance of a main character, then the variety of
automobiles depicted in Trafic actually become characters as
well. It is common for Tati to bring to life inanimate objects while allowing his human characters to fend for themselves. James Monaco wrote:

> The cars and trucks of Traffic are anthropomor-
> phized: they have recognizable facial features and
> body structures; they make interpretable sounds--
> one can tell if they are tired or hungry or happy. [131]

Drivers painfully flex their bodies after the accident. _Trafic_ (1971). (Courtesy Columbia Pictures.)

One is given a panoramic view of a world designed for and
populated by automobiles. Human beings seem to recede to
a secondary position for a number of the film's sequences.
The pivotal scene in the film is an elaborately staged traffic accident involving about a dozen different cars. As each
car hurtles through the smash-up, being struck in one manner or another, it reacts totally differently from every other
car. The movements and sounds of each injured auto are
unique unto themselves.

The auto accident holds the same importance in Trafic that the Royal Garden sequence held in Playtime. Each
of these scenes is built up to during the film and in Playtime's case is a bringing together of the various themes and
in the case of Trafic is the point from which all subsequent
action will grow. Both scenes embody the essence of the
film within their own complex choreography. The auto accident begins when a traffic cop is sent spinning like a top in
the middle of an intersection. Each car, as it hurls into
the crossroads, is sent into a unique skid, slide, crash or
crunch. Tati builds the comedy as each car successively
meets a more and more bizarre fate. A Citroen is sent
skidding with its nose on the ground and its tail end high in
the air. A tiny car ends up spinning in circles like a phonograph record. Tati ends the sequence with a tiny punctuation. A tire knocked loose from a Volkswagen rolls along
the ground. The Volkswagen bounces across the grass,
chasing it, with its front lid snapping open and shut like a
huge mouth. The runaway tire takes a bounce into the air
and neatly lands into the mouth of the pursuing car like a
fly being slurped up by a fat frog. The car's trunk snaps
shut, satisfied. The sequence which began on a small ac-
tion--the cop knocked into a spin--builds through a series of
large-scale stunts to end, again, on this small shot.

The aftermath of the accident is as well thought out
as the accident itself. Tati has all of the drivers slowly
and painfully pull themselves from their damaged cars.
Testing their bodies ever so carefully, they start bending and
flexing and stretching their strained and taxed muscles. In
Tati-esque transposition, the drivers end up standing roughly
in a straight line and appear suddenly to be doing calisthen-
ics in unison. Scattered about the landscape are various
pieces of car wreckage, a headlight here, a bumper there.
The drivers silently start combing the area, staring intently
at the ground. The scene begins to look like some mysterious ritual or, more simply, an Easter egg hunt. When one

of the drivers walks past carrying his rifle, the group suddenly takes on the appearance of a hunting party. Tati, also, experiments with staging these actions in both foreground
and background planes of the scene, simultaneously.

A priest kneels beside the opened hood of his car,
examining parts from its broken engine. As he lifts each
piece into the air for inspection, he appears to be giving
communion while kneeling at the altar of his car. In the
background a small car approaches the scene of the auto
disaster. The car seems to hesitate as it notices the pile
up ahead. It swerves and finally plunges off the road, into
the woods. The bit is played without ever seeing the driver's face, yet it works in transmitting the emotions of confusion and fear through the car's human-like movements.
Hulot runs over to the freshly wrecked car. The driver has
hurt his knee and has difficulty walking. In typical subdued
panic, Hulot runs back to the road for help. Hulot demonstrates the man's limp as he pantomimes the man's predicament to another driver. Hulot continues to limp as he runs
back toward the injured man. It takes a few moments before Hulot remembers that he, himself, is not injured.
From this scene springs the action for the rest of the film.
Hulot must concern himself with getting the injured man
home and then with getting the damaged camping car repaired. One can easily imagine that Tati might have worked
out the gags for this sequence first and then built a film
around it.

Although the structure of the film is a linear one,
perhaps more so than other Tati films, the simple goal of
reaching Amsterdam on time does not deter Tati from pursuing an occasional tangent. None of the characters, be-
sides Maria, seems to feel any urgency to reach the auto
show on time. The adventures along the way are too full
of the real essence of living for anyone to hurry past them.
As Hulot waits for the camping car to be repaired, he
strolls beside a river in the late evening light. A group of
young people sit on a river bank and listen to the sounds of
a guitar. The next day, Marcel, Hulot, Maria and the auto
repairman sit down for a lovely picnic lunch only to be
roused when Maria becomes impatient to get the camper repaired.

Tati's tangents will even lead him away from his own
characters. Indulging in a sequence that is very nearly pure
cinema, Tati films the white highway lines flashing past.

Seated are Marcel (Marcel Fraval), the truck driver; Hulot;
Maria (Maria Kimberly), the P.R. woman; and the garage
owner (Tony Kneppers)--all gathered around the camping car's
pull-out table for an impromptu picnic lunch. Trafic (1971).
(Courtesy Academy Library.)

Using Charles Dumont's upbeat jazz score, Tati synchron-
izes the music to the flashing lines. The intermittent lines
are accompanied by the syncopation of drums; solid lines
produce a sustained organ chord. The technique of match-
ing action directly to the beat of the music, or vice versa,
was used here by Tati for the first time. With a childlike
fascination, Tati shows the distorted reflections of the
speeding lines as they appear in the shiny bumpers and fen-
ders of moving cars. The speed of the lines, along with
the force of the music, heightens the urgency of the group's
reaching Amsterdam. A scene that is not at all a part of
the film's overall movement takes place once the auto show
has been reached. Tati takes to the rainy streets of Amsterdam. Further humanizing the automobile, Tati examines
the peculiar workings of windshield wipers on a variety of

cars caught in a downtown traffic jam. Slowly one realizes
that the movements of the wipers reflect the personality of
the person behind the wheel. Two women sit in their car,
talking energetically back and forth. The wipers flop from
side to side in direct accordance with whichever woman is
speaking. A hippie sits in his jeep, listening to heavy rock
music on the radio. The wipers on his bizarrely decorated
vehicle slide back and forth in a thoroughly erratic manner.
A trembling old man sits huddled behind the wheel of his
car. His wipers slowly and weakly creak back and forth
across his windshield. The tangents and small asides seem
to make up the basis of Tati's films. His works are not
so much story or character as they are simple observation;
the kind of observation that comes usually when Tati pauses
from his storyline to dawdle over some minor point.

     The technique of transposition is, again, evident in
Trafic. One is shown a high angle view of the cars on display at the auto show. An eager group of car buffs crowd
around one car, leaning under its hood for closer inspection. From above, it appears that the entire group is being
swallowed by an animal with a huge and gaping metal mouth.
The transformation of the camping car into a "space capsule," as Maria demonstrates it for the police, is another
obvious example. When one of the Altra company executives
walks through the doors of the auto show, he is followed co-
incidentally by two workmen, each carrying a large potted
palm. The man's simple entrance is transformed into some
grand procession: the king followed by his entourage. These
scenes are all the more amusing because none of the parti-
cipants are even conscious of what is happening. Another,
rather drawn out transposition gag is, perhaps, the weakest
gag in the film. It suffers because the people involved are
aware of what they are doing. Piton, Maria's small and
fluffy dog, is taken from her parked car by a group of mis-
chievous kids and replaced with a similar looking sheepskin
vest. When the vest is placed under one of the car's wheels
with Piton's leash wrapped around it, it appears as if the
dog had been crushed. Maria is grief stricken. Hulot realizes a switch has been made and, in order to show Maria,
yanks on the leash to free the vest from beneath the wheel.
As Hulot tugs harder and harder, Maria shrieks even more
loudly. The scene lacks the impact of other gag sequences
because the audience is forced to watch as the gag is slowly
set up and contrived. There is no sudden and delightful
moment of recognition. The gag also lacks the amusing
quality of having occurred out of sheer chance, spontaneously.

In other scenes, Tati relies less on technique and
more on the character of Hulot. Hulot has driven the injured man home after the auto accident. In order to awaken
the man's wife, Hulot vainly tosses pebbles at her window.
Instead of staging an easy gag like having the window break,
Tati has Hulot climb the ivy-covered facing of the house in
order to reach the window. Only Hulot would take this impractical course of action rather than simply calling for the
man's wife or knocking on the door. Hulot manages to pull
down all the ivy. The man's wife appears at the front door
and escorts her husband inside. Hulot, the gentleman, decides that the only proper thing to do is to pull the ivy back
into its original position. He simply can not leave well
enough alone. Hulot climbs a tree beside the house, slides
out on a limb and attempts to yank the mass of ivy upwards.
Hulot loses his precarious balance, slips and ends swinging
upside down from the tree limb. He dangles quietly, like a
possum, in the darkness. Maria and a young man appear
in the yard below. They do not notice Hulot and he, with
the logic of a guilty child, would rather remain in his ridiculous position than be discovered. The scene becomes funnier when Tati chooses to show it in a wide angle, Hulot at
the upper right and Maria and friend at screen left. By
seeing the relative position of the characters, Hulot's predicament seems all the more absurd. Suddenly, one hears
the sounds of coins hitting the ground. Hulot is losing his
pocket change, followed by the contents of his wallet. The
well-timed use of sound topping off the scene is indicative
of Tati's creativity in that area. The action of this scene
is prompted entirely by Hulot's character. Only Hulot would
have gotten himself into such a predicament and only Hulot
would have remained in it.

Trafic presents a Hulot who is better integrated into
society yet still only half aware of what he is doing. He
always seems to be looking in the wrong direction when he
enters a scene. Outside the garage, Maria discovers her
dead "dog" and lets out a scream. Going to her aid, Hulot
races outside looking off in the wrong direction before realizing Maria is standing behind him. When the Dutch police
inspect the camping car, Hulot, deep in thought, walks towards the sergeant's office to speak with him. Unaware of
what he is doing, Hulot steps through the doorway into the
office, slowly turns around and notices, then, the door
through which he has just passed. He thinks he is now
standing outside the office door and boldly walks through it,
actually stepping back outside again. Hulot almost seems to

be piecing the world together with the very occasional frag-
ments of reality he is witness to.

    As with most of Tati's films, Trafic takes place over
a number of days. Tati shows some clumsiness in his pacing and, consequently, in his handling of the passage of
time. Although Hulot and his crew spend two nights and a
day at the country garage, waiting for the camper to be repaired, Tati condenses and edits the scenes in such a manner that one has no sense of having spent that amount of
time there. One becomes disoriented. One must ask oneself just how long the characters have been on the road.
Tati does not create the feeling of just how near to or far
from reaching his destination Hulot may be. Consequently,
the ending of the film comes too quickly; one has not been
prepared for it. Perhaps, this is one of the difficulties
with a picaresque style of construction. One senses the need
here for the orientation provided by simple mounting action,
climax and denouement.

    Tati's basic subjects of man versus nature, nature
versus technology and gentleness versus harshness are clearly mirrored in both the characterizations and locations of
Trafic. As usual, Tati sets up none of the characters as
villains. The character that most obviously represents the
automobile-oriented mentality is Maria. One may look upon
Maria as an opposing force to Hulot. Can one, then, equate
Maria with Madame and Monsieur Arpel of Mon Oncle? Although Maria and Hulot attempt to reach the same goal, they
go about it very differently. Maria has no time for anyone
or anything that does not help her to reach her goal. On
the other hand, Hulot finds the real value of life in just
those things that may slow down his overall progress. Maria races through the Dutch customs without stopping, she
orders the police around while they inspect the camping car
and, when set free, she drives off so quickly that she causes the big traffic accident that is the film's pivotal point.
It is Maria who disrupts Hulot, Marcel and the car repairman as they pause for a picnic lunch. Hulot, who is more
or less dragged obediently behind Maria, is a character
whose soul is tuned to a very different pace of life. Hulot
appreciates the value of lingering, of leisurely meals with
friends and of strolling by the riverside in the evening.
That Hulot and Maria continue to be friends throughout the
film shows that Tati is not concerned with dramatic conflict,
nor does he pass judgment on his characters.

Tati chose his locations well. By intercutting the
country and the city (represented by the auto show) throughout the film Tati builds his own sense of opposing forces.
The sound of marching music over the loudspeakers is juxtaposed to the natural sounds of the countryside through
which Hulot's party must pass. Sometimes the transition
from country to city can be done by something as simple as
having Hulot running from the highway into the nearest village. The roar of automobiles is then quickly replaced by
the gentle and distant barking of a dog. Creating the oppositions in both locations and characters is about as deep as
Tati will delve into dramatic structure.

When the crew of travelers finally reaches Amsterdam, it is too late. The auto show has just closed. Hulot
is fired on the spot by his irate boss. He prowls around
the deserted convention hall. Outside, on the street, Marcel is desperately demonstrating the camping car to passers-
by. Hulot opens his ever-present umbrella and walks off into the rain. It seems one should have expected Hulot to
end up this way. A man with his set of values will most
always run up against those whose values have been molded
entirely by society. Hulot descends the stairs into a sub-
way station just as a mass of people, all carrying umbrellas, starts up the stairs towards him. His umbrella is
hooked and carried off on top of the rising field of umbrellas. He scurries back up the steps to retrieve it and runs
into Maria. She walks off with Hulot, offering him some
gentle solace. This final moment of tenderness seems out
of place, tacked on and rather forced, even though Tati has
characteristically brought his hero and heroine together at
the film's close. Maria's character has been so business-
like and perfunctory, unlike the gentler women in Tati's
other films, that this display of affection is unrealistic.
Maria is, perhaps, a more modern woman than those seen
in the other films; a representation of her sex's lost gentil-
ity. It is unfortunate that Tati tries, in the end, to fit her
into one of his ready-made molds. Knowing Hulot's gentle
tolerance of the world, one can see him accept the brash
young woman as a friend, but one only wishes Maria were
kept more closely in character. Their final display of
friendship would have meant so much more.

As Maria and Hulot head off into the rain, a number
of cars are snarled in a traffic jam. The camera slowly
zooms out revealing more and more cars brought to a dead
stop. All the drivers have taken to foot and are wending

their way through the vast expanse of stalled machines.
Their tiny upraised umbrellas appear as moving dots across
the shiny, rainsoaked background of cars. James Monaco
has captured the feeling of the film's ending by observing
that "both Traffic and Playtime evoke no hilarious seizures
of guffaws; they are quiet films that end in smiles rather
than belly-laughs."132

    Trafic's reception by the critics was mixed. Coming
after Playtime, the film disappointed many who had secretly
hoped that Tati might just top himself. R. C. Dale has
written that "Traffic is Tati's weakest picture to date."133
By comparison, he goes on to describe Playtime as not only
Tati's best film, but one of the best films of the 1960's.
Dale also reiterated the more common complaints among
the critics. The film was considered poorly paced, not
developing a rhythm of its own. It was felt that Tati had
not created any interesting relationships between his characters. Dale was left with the impression that Trafic
was hastily put together and that Tati obviously lacked the
time he required to slowly develop and test each of his
gags.

    The film was anxiously received in America, but by a
much smaller audience than had seen Tati's earlier films.
Trafic failed to generate the following that Les Vacances and
Mon Oncle had enjoyed. Despite the slower pace of Trafic
and the transparency of some of its gags, it is an entertaining and occasionally profound comedy. Tati does not always
go for the big laugh. Trafic, in most of its sequences,
deals with the tiny details that Tati finds fascinating. Trafic is best viewed when one expects to be treated to no
more than a series of eccentric looks at one's own style of
living. In Trafic's start and stop pace, full of disgressions,
one senses a lighter-weight film than the earlier works,
which may have bowled over their audiences by the sheer
pace and volume of their gags. Trafic's validity is not les-
sened by these differences, however.

CHAPTER 10

TATI'S FILMS
AS A REACTION TO THE NEW WORLD

Tati has been attacking the way one perceives one's
world as much as he has been satirizing the world itself.
All of Tati's films, whether Hulot is present in a scene or
not, manifest the startled and objective point of view of Hulot. It takes a slightly mad character like Hulot to stumble
beyond society's carefully drawn guidelines and to see things
with a rare objectivity. By narrowing the scope of one's
perceptions, by leaving the mechanics of the world unana-
lyzed and unquestioned, one can force the world into an appearance of sanity. Consequently, few people allow themselves the honesty of Hulot's perceptions as the systems and
procedures of the world move in too close to be seen. Tati's comedy hits home because his insights deal with the
common reality of automobiles, highways, skyscrapers and
garbage disposals.

Tati's satire on contemporary life is characterized by
his optimism. In making fun of society's foibles, a subject
where pessimism runs rampant, Tati maintains a sympathe-
tic understanding for all his characters. He sees everyone
as a victim, one way or another, of society's misplaced values. It does not matter to Tati whether one is on the receiving or the giving end of society's dictates. As much
sympathy is shown to the well-established Arpels in Mon Oncle as is shown to Hulot. Unlike Chaplin, Tati does not
rely upon pathos. It is not necessary for the audience to
pity Hulot or feel hatred for his opponents. Hulot's actual
adversaries are not the people who drive the big automobiles
or inhabit the skyscrapers, but are, rather, the systems
themselves and the narrow-mindedness that allows them.
Most everyone falls victim to these systems and has to compromise just a little of their essential humanity in order to
keep functioning in society. Obviously, Hulot resists the
compromise.

Hulot is an eccentric because he operates outside the system. Even while working for the car company in Trafic Hulot seems to hold little stake in the job. When fired at the end of the film, he does not protest, he simply walks off. No grief is displayed and, most likely, none is felt. Bitterness is not an element in Tati's films.

Is there despair behind Hulot's nearly unshakeable facade? One feels that there has to be. The world seems to crash in around Hulot's ears as he tries to make his simple way through it. He is, however, little bothered by the senselessness of many of the world's problems. He simply takes it all in stride, expecting no more from life than it is known to give. Consequently, Hulot is forever wary. He has been snapped at often enough by the world's various traps that he expects the next potential disaster to be just around the corner. At the same time, it is Hulot's total willingness to participate in life that marks him as an optimist.

Hulot does not seem to believe that the world is going to get any better. He does believe, however, that one should make the most of one's life in this best of all possible worlds. Obviously, Tati, who satirizes the social structures, does not look at the world and advocate political revolt. When Tati describes himself as having anarchistic tendencies, he is emphasizing a revolt of the human spirit. Hulot's revolt against the order of things is accidental, unintentional and a direct manifestation of his individuality. Whenever Hulot catches a glimpse of his outsider's position, it is his sudden desire to fit in with the world that points out the absurdities of conformity. Hulot is like a child whose own natural, unbridled behavior reminds others of the healthy reactions they may have long since forgotten.

Tati seems superbly equipped for lampooning the foolishness of this over-industrialized epoch. His eye has been sharpened and his comedy nurtured in this world of dehumanizing architecture, inefficient transportation and useless gadgetry. Penelope Gilliatt wrote that "no other director has ever pitted the still small voice of human contact so delicately against the nerveless dominion of modern conveniences."[134] The Arpels in Mon Oncle are seen as victims of their own over-gadgeted lifestyle. Little Gérard and Hulot aptly represent here that "small voice of human contact." It is Hulot's example that wins a small victory for human values by forcing Arpel closer to his son at the end of the film.

There is no more apparent trademark of an era than
its architecture. Architectural and design styles in this era
are what manage to keep people apart. It is only through
the destruction of the Royal Garden nightclub, near the end
of Playtime, that the various characters are brought together. The cold, unfeeling structures of Tati's Paris have
stood in the way of people's natural inclinations. R. C.
Dale observed that, to Tati, the contemporary city is

> a place of buildings that are simply too big for
> their inhabitants, buildings run by machines, in
> which man can do little but get in the way of the
> machines and architecture.[135]

Dale goes on to comment upon Tati's optimistic outlook,
comparing his vision of the modern world with the pessimis-
tic outlook seen in Fritz Lang's brilliant filmic settings.

The camping car in Trafic seems to serve the same
purpose as the crumbling Royal Garden nightclub. Both
have served in their own ways to keep people apart. Dehumanizing architecture and space-capsuled automobiles have
been designed for everyone by those unaware of the importance of human contact. It is not until the elaborately designed camping car is damaged that the many characters in
the film actually come together. It seems to Tati that
chaos is a much more humanizing and more natural state
than coldly and logically conceived order.

Tati is able to look about and see that people are
products of the world that has been designed for them.
One's own architecture, transportation and pace of life directly affect one's personality. Isolation is encouraged in
the design of people's homes and in the dominance of the
automobile as a form of transportation. Normal social in-
terchange is discouraged in a world that does not have the
time to dawdle. Tati feels that the connections between humans start to dissolve when people become remote from
what is designed for them. Natural human instincts are
subjugated to merciless efficiency. People are less and
less in control of their own world as they allow it to become more complicated and unmanageable. Tati warmly
portrays the characters in his films who are willing and
able to fix their machinery with their own hands and are
able, therefore, to maintain some control over that area of
their lives. The comic garage keeper in Trafic who re-
pairs the dent in the camping car and grunts proudly, "I fix

everything," is just such a person. Tati has himself stated:
"I'm always trying to defend the simple man who tries to
fix something with his hands."136

Underlying Tati's absurd universe is the implication
that everyone is a pawn in some global chess game played
by fools. The fact that so many people unthinkingly allow
themselves to be part of that game is ample motivation for
Tati's filmic satire. One must then ask who the people in
control are and what one must do to recapture control over
one's life. Tati does not pretend to have the answers to
these questions. He has simply observed that

> the ones in charge will saturate us, they'll do
> more and more each time. The more they speak
> on television, the more ridiculous they are.137

Tati's outlook on society as a world full of victims rather
than a world full of villains is a sign of his affection toward
people in general, as well as an indication he does not know
who the real villains are. There seems to be no one to
single out. Not even Arpel, who runs a plastics factory, is
treated with anything less than sympathy. Tati does not
pass judgment on any of his characters. He feels that in
his films he "would like to make people smile and give them
a choice."138 The goal seems simple enough. After seeing
a Tati film, one is left with the sense that everyone is, indeed, responsible for the complexities of his own life. Perhaps everyone is a villain. Like Hulot in Trafic, one has
found it necessary to become part of the order of things,
regardless of where one's heart may lie, in order to sur-
vive. If the flowerlike patterns of streetlamps can still be
noticed; if quiet moments of human interaction can be culti-
vated; if dogs are allowed to run free and boys still play
their guitars, then humanity has not given up its rights to
lead fulfilling lives.

Tati sees the modern world as one designed for the
few. He has stated that

> you may have thirty-five boys and girls in a school
> and modern life is made only for the top four.
> They are the inventors, the engineers. The others
> have only to follow, to push buttons.139

Hulot serves as an example of a human being who reacts
against this insidious programming. Hulot demonstrates that

it is still possible to maintain one's own brand of independence. One need not so much rebel directly against the structures of society as simply uphold one's identity. The pressure to conform is great. If society's idea of variety is an auto show full of identical looking cars, then one must accept that maintaining one's independence in that society will cause certain tensions. Hulot, himself, has developed a Buddhalike approach to the difficulties life tends to toss in his eccentric path. Perhaps, the fiercely but quietly independent Hulot is an example for everyone to follow in his or her unique way. In a society which typically refuses to take responsibility for itself and the things it creates and which refuses to admit to the human consequences of its follies, this may be the only way to preserve one's humanity.

CHAPTER 11

TATI'S FILMS
AS A REFLECTION OF THE OLD WORLD

Hulot maintains his unique outlook on contemporary
life through his identification with Old World values. He is
an embodiment of manners, customs and styles of dress
from past generations. The very style and pace of Tati's
films, in addition to their content, display an affinity for
not only an older style of living but for an older style of
filmmaking as well. One of the reasons Tati's films are
so difficult to categorize is precisely this distance they take
from any contemporary style. It is through Tati's eyes,
oriented to the past, that one gets to view, a bit more objectively, one's own world.

The rumpled overcoat, jaunty hat, long-stemmed pipe
and ever-present umbrella all serve to make Hulot stand out from
the more contemporary-looking masses. The umbrella which
serves as a walking stick is a throwback to an era when a
man was not completely dressed until he had his walking
stick in hand. The hat and coat all lend Hulot the air of
polish, albeit slightly rumpled, that most people have long
since found unnecessary. People have more and more discarded all that is not thoroughly pragmatic or essential.
Taking pleasure in doing simple things (dressing up, taking
an evening stroll, lingering over a meal with friends) has
become a less familiar part of life to all but Hulot. It is
obvious also that Hulot's very movements are those from another era. He moves at his own pace, either more slowly
or more quickly than those around him. In Les Vacances,
it is the competitive Hulot who races about in long determined strides from one activity to another while his companions sit back and stare at him disbelieving. In Playtime, it
is a more distracted and overwhelmed Hulot who moves more
slowly than the urgently scurrying masses in the streets.

Even in the modern world of Mon Oncle, with shiny cars
and electric garage doors, Hulot travels by bicycle. Penelope Gilliatt has noted:

> Bicycles also meet a certain stateliness in his
> style and a certain disinclination for any vehicle
> that outsizes the human frame. You feel that he
> much detests the shiny cars of 'My Uncle.' He
> prefers doughnut carts and horse-drawn wagons. [140]

Older and gentler values seem constantly crowded
out in Tati's films. He allows but fleeting glimpses of the
way it used to be. The calm and beautiful moments of
Trafic are usually interrupted by Maria's impatient entreat-
ies. The glimpses of the old Paris in Playtime last no
longer than it takes for a glass door to swing closed. The
scarcity of these moments makes them all the more attractive and their placement in relation to the contemporary
scenes creates a heightened sense of the disparity between
old and new. The sequences in Mon Oncle pertaining to
Hulot's old quarter of the city are far more than just
glimpses of the older world. They are long enough to
stand as opposing elements to the carefully drawn lifestyle
of the Arpels. However, the atmosphere of the old quarter
is colored by the foreboding images of the wrecker's ball
and demolition equipment that open the film. One senses
here that one is watching something whose existence is only
transitory. A brilliant scene from Playtime that embodies
not only the tentative grip one may have on the older ways
of life, but the value one places on them as well, pictures
an oldfashioned lady flower vender among the glass and
steel towers of modern Paris. Tourists crowd around the
woman, vainly trying to snap pictures, hoping to capture a
rare glimpse of the Paris they had dreamed of seeing. The
flower vender, of course, appears thoroughly out of place
and the tourists are unable to catch a snapshot without
someone crowding in the way.

Tati's female characters are portrayed with a rare,
old-style sensitivity. The women are all young and beautiful and, with the exception of Maria in Trafic, are all shyly quiet. Hulot's relationship to each of the female leads
is always a little distant and very proper. There are never
any suspicions of ulterior motives. There really are no
romances in Tati's films, just innocent affections. Hulot
feels great affection for the landlord's daughter in Mon Oncle and taps her gently on the nose each time he sees her.

Giving the little gifts to Barbara in Playtime or shyly escorting Martine in Les Vacances are actions befitting Hulot's concept of women. To Hulot's way of seeing things, women are to be treated gently, respectfully, as if they were special. It is the rather forced affectionate ending to Trafic, with Hulot suddenly arm-in-arm with Maria, that indicates Tati's continued and persistent oldfashioned respect for women.

The view of the world shown in Tati's work is essentially optimistic. The easy and uninspired sarcasm possible in any examination of contemporary society is, instead, replaced by the warm satire of Tati's observations. Tati's obvious sentimentality is not uncomfortable; it works because of the depth and intensity of his humor. R. C. Dale called Tati an "optimist" and "a rather guarded sentimentalist"[141] who chooses to permit us to try to see what touches him, without laying it out explicitly.

Tati's respect for past values is evident, not only in the content of each film but in the very structure of the film. Just as Hulot enjoys the discursive, rambling journey to Amsterdam in Trafic, so Tati enjoys the nonlinear structure of his own films. To Tati the style and process of one's life is as important as the goals one may be struggling to attain. The pauses and asides that make up his films offer more truth and insight than any final resolutions the films may reach. Within this structure, the importance of physical comedy, the gag for the sake of the gag and the use of music and sound effects supplanting dialogue lends Tati's work the frivolous and unpretentious quality of many silent comedies. Penelope Gilliatt wrote that while the Arpels "represent a new order of happiness, Hulot represents the old disorder."[142] It is Tati the filmmaker who expresses this "old disorder" through the spontaneous and impulsive construction of his films.

If Playtime is placed last among the order of Tati's films, as Tati requests, one starts to notice the diminishing of Old World elements throughout his films. The sleepy country village of Jour de Fête is totally lost in the distance by the time Playtime arrives. The seaside village in Les Vacances invaded by the city folk, the sequences in Mon Oncle depicting Hulot's old quarter of the city and the seesawing back and forth between countryside and city in Trafic can all be considered intermediate steps to the ultimate disappearance of one's heritage. The oldfashioned gracefulness which formed the environment of Tati's earlier films is reduced to fleeting reflections in the plate glass of Playtime. Tati's constant references back to the older order of things, no matter how concise, tend to nudge the audience back into brief moments of lucidity. If Old World values are being crowded out in Tati's filmic world, one can rest assured that at least they will continue in the person of Hulot.

CHAPTER 12

TATI'S UNIVERSE

André Bazin has stated that if Tati's vision of things is amusing and if the character of Hulot is amusing, as well, it is "almost accessorily or at any rate always relative to the universe."143 In comedy a universe must be created and agreed upon between creator and audience in order for the comedy to work. To shift from one established comic style to another within a film is disorienting and disturbing. Characters playing slapstick can not suddenly be seen to injure themselves in a realistic fall. Likewise, the characters of a more realistic comedy can not be given the acrobatic, almost supernatural agility shown in slapstick performances. When the style of a comedy is inconsistent in this manner it points out the artificiality of the entire production. Once the filmmaker has gotten the audience's implicit agreement to pretend what is on the screen is reality, the filmmaker betrays his own film if he admits to any other reality. If, for example, Tati were to introduce into one of his films a character who speaks as clearly and as often as a normal person, the artifice of Tati's near speechless world would be exposed. It is, therefore, essential that within these agreements and within the style of characterization and prescribed distance from reality no inconsistencies be allowed. Unlike many contemporary filmmakers, Tati has been able to build a solid and functioning universe. It is the resonating quality of that peculiar universe that lasts long after one has forgotten the many gags in a Tati film. Tati's universe is as unique as Chaplin's or Keaton's.

Jonathan Rosenbaum has eloquently expressed a sense of Tati's comic universe:

> Like all of the very great comics, before making us laugh, Tati creates a universe. A world ar-

ranges itself around his character.... He can be
personally absent from the most comical gags,
for M. Hulot is only the metaphysical incarnation
of a disorder that is perpetuated long after his
passing. 144

That Hulot is able to be absent from entire sections of Tati's films is evidence that the comic universe holds up by
itself. No comedy film could maintain itself for long by
focusing on the actions of ordinary people, as Tati chooses
to do, without first having a comedy framework or a universe into which to place these people and their activities.

The delicately delineated universe of Les Vacances
adds dimension to many of the film's simple gags. Hulot's
presence creates a certain quiet fear and insanity among
the guests at the seaside hotel. When Hulot, driving down
the street in his backfiring car, almost runs over a woman
who is walking her dog, she yanks the dog out of the way
at the last instant. She then crosses the street and goes
out of frame. From offscreen one hears another squeal of
brakes from another car. The woman then reappears,
clutching her dog in her arms, racing madly down the
street. It is as if the cumulative effect of Hulot's personality is so great that people around him are constantly tee-
tering on the brink of insanity. Hulot affects most of the
other characters in similar ways. Some are closer to the
edge than others, for example, the two taciturn hotel keepers who manage occasionally to slip over into Hulot's crazi-
ness despite their quiet dislike for him. One of the hotel
keepers observes Hulot making faces in the mirror and becomes so fascinated by this that he unconsciously joins in.
When he spills the beer he is carrying, he is snapped back
to reality. Another time, the man is so distracted by Hulot's own disorientation that when a guest greets him he
turns and mistakenly greets the guest's reflection in the
glass dining room door. It is precisely these odd character
ticks and reactions that make up the fabric of the comedy
universe in Tati's films.

The ever-suffering hotel keepers of Les Vacances
manifest themselves in characters from other Tati films.
The slowly moving, dog-faced, young mechanic who makes
a brief and disgruntled appearance in Trafic embodies a
similar, rather negative outlook on life. What one begins
to realize is that nowhere in Tati's films are there characters that are any heavier than these. Tati may use charac-

ters to establish a counterpoint or to set up a conflict in
his simple story structure, but he never lays blame on or
shows antagonism toward any of his characters. The audience, like Tati, does not insist there be a villain who is
defeated. Unlike Chaplin or Keaton, Hulot's success is
based upon other, simpler victories. Tati shows certain
characters to be foolish, but all in the light of understanding. Hulot's victory is simply that he survives in this
world. Tati's universe may be full of characters who lack
any perspective on themselves, such as the Arpels and Maria, but none of them are seen as evil.

This filmic universe is quite similar, in many ways,
to the real world. If there are no clear-cut villains depicted here, one must realize that there are few unmistakably,
clear-cut villains in the world. Tati's universe parallels
the real world. He concerns himself with everyday activities. Basil Wright observed of Hulot:

> It is from his reality that the funniness arises,
> the extraordinary things which happen to him are
> only too possible. They could happen to anyone.
> Only occasionally does Tati put things to a
> stretch. [145]

Tati himself has commented upon his selection of characters
and what they contribute to his own view of the world:

> I saw the other day the real people who played in
> the restaurant in Playtime, and I'm sure that ten
> years from now, a waiter will still be the same....
> I think Playtime will be better a few years from
> now when more and more people have received the
> new decor in their lives. [146]

Tati has typically chosen to explore public behavior
rather than the internal workings of one single character.
Crowds and masses of people seem to dominate Tati's films.
He rarely lingers on one character, including Hulot, for very
long. The personalities of various locations also dominate
the film. The Arpels' house, the quaint Hôtel de la Plage,
the Royal Garden nightclub and the crowded Dutch highways
all play major "roles" in various Tati films. Tati feels
that the settings of his films are as much the stars as any
other element. In fact they have become more and more
dominant. Roy Armes stated that as a result "the exaggeration inevitably associated with a comic character is thus

pushed into the background and gives place to a more realistic portrayal of life."[147] Tati's concern with setting is
so great that he had, at one time, planned to base an entire film around the life of a single town. The film, to
have been entitled, simply, The Town, would have been
comprised of a series of stories, each presenting a different aspect of the town. If, in Tati's films, there appears
to be less and less of a main character for one to identify
with, it is simply Tati's democracy at work, allowing the
audience to choose which actions and which characters it
will follow.

        The inanimate object seems to play a very important
role in Tati's universe. Interest in the personalities of
many of the autos in Trafic surpasses even that generated
by many of the film's human characters. In Les Vacances,
Hulot's sputtering Amilcar is so closely associated with his
own personality that the lengthy opening sequence of the film
introduces him solely through the personality of his car.
The incredible array of gadgets in the Arpel household
serves to add much of the character to the film Mon Oncle.
The wheezing chairs in the waiting room in Playtime display a near human awareness of what goes on around them.
Tati emphasizes the behavioral characteristics of machines
to the point of rendering them absurd. The docile and so-
ber reactions of the film's characters become also absurd
by comparison and one is, as a result, quickly able to see
the foolishness of one's own compliant reactions to the dehumanizing factors in the real world.

        When examining the comic universes of various classic
film comedians, one realizes that no matter how realistically or fancifully drawn a universe may be, it must always be
drawn in a style that can contain the personality of the particular clown to be placed within it. No matter how broad
Chaplin's filmic character may have been in comparison to
most of the other characters in his films, there were always
villains and heroines as extreme in their portrayals as Chaplin was in his. Chaplin needed the menacing figure of an
oversized Eric Campbell or the helpless and forsaken Edna
Purviance; Chaplin could not have existed in Tati's universe,
he was conditioned for different challenges. Likewise, one
imagines with a shudder the inadequacies of Hulot's character if he were ever forced to deal with the open villainy of
Chaplin's universe. Keaton's universe is much closer to
that of Tati's. Keaton allows the inanimate object a full
range of behavior. Like Tati, Keaton insists that his sup-

porting characters be played realistically. Lloyd, as well, will assign the greatest potential to inanimate objects and to his ability to deal with them, although he does not approach them analytically. Lloyd's human characters are similarly lifelike. Keaton and Lloyd chose to push characterization into the background for the sake of dealing with objects. Tati's universe falls neatly in line, in its own way, with these earlier filmic visions.

Tati is aware that the odd and specifically drawn universe of his films may not appeal to everyone. He has commented accurately that:

> Either you accept it or you don't; if it's not your visual idea of yourself, you leave the cinema after a quarter of an hour. If you like it, understand it, it's like impressionist painting, you find more in it to interest you--sound, movement, people--when you go back to it. [148]

The insight one may gather from Hulot's activities would not exist if Hulot were part of another universe. As a living character, Hulot is only possible within his universe. The eccentricity of Tati's constructed universe is such that Hulot may, perhaps, be the only silent clown who would have no chance at all of surviving anywhere else.

CHAPTER 13

TATI'S COMEDY STYLE

Tati never breaks the rules of his carefully constructed universe, but he does stretch them to their limits for best comic effect. Against the realistic backdrops of Tati's films, a sudden intricately choreographed traffic pile-up or an inanimate object's surprisingly human reactions may push the limits of credibility. Tati is, however, aware of those limits and plays within their boundaries. Tati has allowed himself enough room, within the boundaries of his universe, to suddenly push an action or a performance a step further and surprise his audience. If one thinks one is watching Giffard chase Hulot in Playtime, one is surprised to find that it is Hulot's reflection he has been chasing. The Arpels caught in their garage in Mon Oncle is a mildly amusing situation until Tati pushes the scene a step further by having the garage door turn into the huge, round-eyed face of a monster. The traffic accident in Trafic, as well, is taken beyond its common quality when the damaged cars start acting like dying animals. Few, if any, of the actions performed by man or machine in a Tati film are impossible; one of Tati's understandings with his audience is that he will operate within the physical laws of the real world. If conditions are just right, any number of Tati's seemingly fantastic gags could, indeed, take place. It is this constant pressure against and exploration within the limits of his universe that endows Tati's films with such unpredictable and freewheeling qualities.

One quiet but typical scene from Mon Oncle has Hulot, at work in the plastics factory, taking a moment to squat down and pet the factory dog. The dog gets up and walks away. Arpel appears and, naturally, wonders just what Hulot is doing squatting on the ground. Of course, Hulot has no explanation. The situation is extremely funny and peculiarly simple. One can hardly imagine such a minimal

127

gag, if it can be termed a gag at all, as a part of anyone
else's film. Cauliez has observed that story, characters,
decor and staging are less essential to Tati than a delicately crafted "comic disposition."149

          Tati follows through on every moment of his films to
their full comedy potential, even to the point of belaboring
some scenes. His films, therefore, tend to be discursive,
pausing over certain details and rushing off along tangents
that often lead away from Hulot himself. Resisting the dictates of a dramatically structured plot, Tati chooses to linger where he likes. Tati develops gags within predeter-
mined characters, well before he calls in assistance from
any screenwriters. What results, according to Walter Kerr's
terminology, are a series of "charm-bracelet films"150
with one gag strung to the next with rather thin plot material. Tati's comedies can also be seen as picaresque tales.
As do the characters of Don Quixote or Huckleberry Finn,
Hulot serves as the one unifying element in the story. Gerald Mast's description of the picaresque character applies
directly to Hulot. He feels the central character must be
one

          whose function is to bounce off the people and
          events around him, often, in the process, reveal-
          ing the superiority of his comic bouncing to the
          social and human walls he hits.151

          One can detect Tati's early music hall experience in
his approach to story material. The style of much of Tati's
stage work was based simply upon funny gags and not upon
carefully plotted material. Cauliez said that

          a gag for Tati is not a number, an attraction, an
          hors-d'oeuvre; it is an abridged situation, a film-
          within-a-film--but a brief film compared to the
          entire film, a cell in a tissue.152

Gerald Mast would agree with this observation. Mast feels
that, while Tati's style of comedy can be seen as picaresque, he employs a "riffing" technique, as well. Riffing, a
musical term, applies here to Tati's exploitation of all the
gags found possible within any given situation or with any
given object. In Les Vacances, the succession of things that
happen to Hulot in Martine's living room, while waiting to
take her riding, is an example of riffing within a certain
location. The auto show in Trafic is also a scene that is

thoroughly "riffed." The multifaceted camping car is the
most obvious example of Tati's riffing technique applied to
a single object. With the use of this technique, one can
see still another comparison between Tati's films and the
early films of Chaplin.

Tati employs a variety of different types of gags
throughout his films. Some gags start with a moment of
confusion: a seemingly nonsensical action is seen to take
place. The audience is disoriented until Tati swiftly reveals what is going on. The exercising vacationers, on the
beach in Les Vacances, strenuously hold a deep knee bend
position for a longer and longer amount of time. One starts
to wonder why they all maintain such a strenuous position
until the camera reveals that Hulot has distracted the attention of the exercise leader from his class. The pay-off is
simple--a baffling action followed by a simple explanation.
The scene from Trafic where the auto show officials stretch
string across the convention hall floor is a reversal of the
pay-off gag format. Instead of showing a mysterious and
unexplainable action first and then revealing the explanation,
Tati first shows the explanation, the men stretching the
strings, and then shows the mysterious looking result: the
odd high-stepping dance of the officials. The outcome of
the situation in this case is more of a pay-off than is the
underlying explanation.

Naturally, many of Tati's pay-off gags can not be set
up in a few simple shots, as those mentioned above. Many
gags must build to their pay-off through a number of elaborate steps. The best gags are such that one never realizes a gag is being constructed until it is actually sprung.
Hulot found hanging upside down in a tree, in Trafic, is the
unexpected pay-off for a detailed gag. The lengthy gag designed to fool Maria into believing her dog was run over is,
however, an example of a gag that develops too slowly and
with too much contrivance to surprise the audience with an
unexpected pay-off.

Stanley Kauffmann has pointed out that Tati will, occasionally, disregard a gag's pay-off altogether. In the
Royal Garden sequence from Playtime, a series of eager
waiters seasons and reseasons a platter of fish on its way
to the table. "But," complains Kauffmann, "by now the
first pair of diners have moved to another table. The fish
is wheeled away to their new table and we never see the
pay-off."153

Sprinkled throughout Tati's films are one-shot gags.
These, the simplest of all gags, are usually developed by
the careful placement of the subject within a single shot.
A number of the gags in Trafic's auto show are just such
bits. The overhead shot of people leaning under a car's
opened hood appears to show a giant animal gulping down
its victims. And, as mentioned before, in Playtime, Tati
placed a minister in front of a neon "Drugstore" sign so
that the "O" appears as a halo directly behind his head.

Armes has said of Tati that "his sense of timing is
one of his greatest assets."[154] Much of Hulot's character
is formed by his slow perceptions and quick physical reactions. The running gag depicting the dripping taffy in Les
Vacances is effective because of Tati's sense of timing.
He is able to walk past the taffy, take a moment for his
perceptions to register and then twist instantly in a circle,
lunging out to save the gooey mass. In another small bit
from the same film, Hulot again approaches the hotel's front
door. Instead of being distracted by the taffy, he almost
runs straight into one of the hotel keepers, a character who
greatly intimidates Hulot. Without even breaking stride,
Hulot nimbly twirls about and continues walking off in another direction. In Mon Oncle, Hulot wends his way acro-
batically through the Arpel's front yard garden decorations.
The gracefulness of his movements is enhanced by his
sense of timing. Hulot has the ability to almost tip over
the brink of disaster and then save himself at the last,
carefully chosen instant. The crashing flag pole in the
early Jour de Fête is funny precisely because of the lightning speed with which François appears at the upstairs window of the house into which the pole falls. Tati carries
remnants of this into Les Vacances, producing one of the
film's funniest running gags: Hulot will disappear into the
hotel and instantly pop his head out his attic window only
seconds after causing some form of havoc. The speed with
which he accomplishes this act, coupled with his innocent
nonchalance, produces an hilarious effect.

Hulot's pacing is integral to his character. He walks
with long, bouncing strides, quite apart from the pace of
movement shown by those around him. His head jerks from
side to side like a chicken as he investigates whatever situation is at hand. He nods his head curtly in acceptance or
in response to whatever he has been considering. Like the
great silent clowns, especially Keaton, Hulot operates within the laws of the real world. It is his balletic ability in

dealing with that real world and in moving his gangling
frame out of danger's path that is so delightful to watch.

Penelope Gilliatt has said of comedy:

> Maybe all funniness has a tendency to throw set-
> tled things into doubt. Where most people will
> automatically complete an action, a great come-
> dian will stop in the middle to have a think about
> the point of it, and the point will often vanish be-
> fore our eyes. [155]

Hulot never quite understands the reasons behind people's
activities but, with the childlike enthusiasm of a Harry
Langdon, joins in obediently. Like a child who has discovered something new, Hulot's compulsive shaking of hands
and his briskly proper bows prompt one to re-examine these
activities with a new objectivity. Unlike Chaplin, Hulot
rarely distances himself far enough from what he is doing
to be able to look objectively upon his activity. Hulot becomes far more engrossed in what he does than the ever-
playful Chaplin.

As a matter of course, Tati fills his universe with
gadgets designed outlandishly enough to be just implausible.
A push broom equipped with headlights for sweeping in dark
places is obviously a joke, but just barely so. How many
of one's own appliances are similar? The housewares show
in Playtime is much the same as the auto show in Trafic:
concentrated within one location are samples of technology's
latest offerings. The tourists in Playtime, along with the
incredulous Hulot, crowd around the displays of such necessary items as doors designed to slam silently closed and
women's glasses with lenses that flip up separately so that
eye make-up may be applied. The many devices that make
up Madame Arpel's stylishly appointed kitchen are fine examples of foolishly over-efficient appliances. As early as
Jour de Fête, Tati's characters were enamored of newfan-
gled devices and modern gizmos. François was fascinated
by the latest and most efficient postal techniques and even
went as far as to have a telephone mounted on the handle-
bars of his bicycle.

Most of Tati's characters are so deeply involved in
society's many conventions or customs that they begin to
take them seriously. Madame Arpel, in Mon Oncle, is a
prime example. On the other hand, it is Hulot's naive and

Hulot, wandering about a housewares show, is about to be
shown the latest thing: doors that slam silently. <u>Playtime</u>
(1967). (Courtesy French Film Office.)

---

wide-eyed reactions to the world that make its gadgetry and
its accepted ways of doing things appear so suddenly ridiculous. Hulot essentially represents everyone's own secret
instincts as he causes havoc in Madame Arpel's meticulously designed, space-age kitchen. To the degree that one remains out of touch with one's rather natural inclinations,
one is like the Arpels. Hulot's unabashed naturalness easily exposes the pointlessness behind many accepted activities.
Hulot simply takes the time to look for the point in the
first place.

Tati relies heavily upon the intelligence and perceptions of those he is playing to. Unlike conventional comedy,
Tati does not force the audience's attention to one particular
gag. While he may stage a number of gags simultaneously,
he allows the audience to focus on that which interests them
the most. The many ongoing activities in the Royal Garden
restaurant scene serve as a major example. The aftermath

of the auto wreck in Trafic is also an instance of multi-layered activity. Hulot may be the focus of attention at the top of the frame as he walks across the hill but, at the same time, the lower portion of the frame is occupied by people scavenging for the pieces of their shattered cars. Within the crowded wide shots of the scene one can pick out any character or action one wishes. The approach of the final, lone auto is seen only in the distance. As the car swerves off the road and into the woods one can just as easily be observing some other activity.

Tati is quite content to set up situations that are paid off simply in smiles. The world's mildly amusing idiosyncracies are as valid an area of attention for Tati as are hilariously elaborate gags. One of the sour-faced hotel keepers of Les Vacances, in attempting to free his hands to carry a tray, ends up placing Hulot's hat on his head and gripping Hulot's pipe in his teeth. The situation is not hilarious, it is, however, amusing to see the hotel keeper momentarily transposed into Hulot. The American businessman's cold and constant stare at the hotel keepers is another example of an idiosyncracy used to full comic potential. Later in the film, one watches from a high angle shot as a little boy crosses the road and heads toward the beach. Suddenly, from offscreen, a band of nearly a dozen small children appear and follow the first one. The sudden shift from a quiet, lonely little scene into a boisterously crowded one is startling in an amusing way. Again, Tati has set up a situation that appears to be one thing and, in a startling moment, becomes something quite different. In Trafic, Maria is constantly accompanied by her little dog Piton who faithfully enters each scene a few moments after she. Each time the little dog slowly enters a scene, dragging its leash behind, one is amused in a small way. In Playtime Tati briefly introduces another character, dressed exactly like Hulot, who wanders about through the housewares show. As with the hotel keeper, the mere idea of there being anyone else in the world who looks like Hulot is quietly amusing. Tati is willing to go for the smaller moments of humor and, in so doing, further demonstrates how tiny moments of comedy abound in life.

In addition to tiny gags, there are scenes in Tati's comedies in which hardly anything funny happens at all. In Les Vacances one watches a couple of little boys eat ice cream cones. The cute scene provides a much needed pause in the film's profusion of gags. The syncopated flashing

Gallant Hulot kicking an assumed Peeping Tom. Les Vacances (1953). (Courtesy Academy Library.)

highway lines in Trafic provide a break, as well, from the
pure gags of the rest of the film. When Martine looks out
her window, down at the beach in Les Vacances, she sees
below her a single person doing exercises and a couple of
beach tents swaying all about as they are being erected,
with the people setting them up invisible inside. The tents
wiggle like fat beached whales. This peaceful, early morning scene is a fascinating combination of elements but is
not particularly humorous.

Common to Tati's style of comedy is the technique
of transposition, mentioned earlier. Seeing an object or an
activity as something totally unrelated is the principle behind Hulot's collapsed kayak looking like the jaws of a large
fish. In Les Vacances, as well, Hulot's runaway car tire
becomes a funeral wreath as its sticky surface picks up
leaves along the ground. The Arpel's infamous garage door
is slickly transposed into a face with two big eyes. Hulot,
asleep in the plastics factory, allows the precious plastic
tubing to ooze from the machine in the erratic shape of link
sausages, to Arpel's dismay and the dog's delight. Playtime's tiny office cubicles appear to be a complicated maze
in which Hulot and Giffard chase about blindly. The endlessly anthropomorphic automobiles of Trafic are probably the
most plentiful examples of transposition in any of Tati's
works. When one of the damaged cars is towed roughly into a nearby garage one hears, in a sound overlay, the car's
painfully human "oohing" and "aahing."

Tati also relies upon natural coincidence to support
many of his gags. An example is the scene, in Les Vacances, where Hulot, fresh from causing some catastrophe,
starts painting a beached kayak in order to appear innocently
occupied. The perfectly timed sweeping in and out of the
waves allows a floating paint can to precisely meet Hulot's
paint brush each time he lowers it for more paint. Later
in the film, Hulot observes what he assumes to be one of
the tourists on the beach bending forward and peeking into a
woman's dressing room. The man is actually standing beyond the dressing room and is bending forward to peer into
his camera for a family snapshot. The gag is simply based
upon a coincidence of position. From Hulot's vantage point
the man appears to be a shameless Peeping Tom and fully
deserves the kick in the rear end that Hulot administers.
The structure of Playtime is built upon coincidence. It is
Hulot's accidental meeting up with the band of lady tourists,
time and time again, that spirals the film towards its cli-

Coincidence, a major element of Tati's humor, causes Hulot to appear to be arresting the police officer. <u>Trafic</u> (1971). (Courtesy Columbia Pictures.)

mactic scene. When Hulot finally meets Giffard, it is by
pure coincidence, as well. A small, but amusing gag from
Trafic, based upon coincidence, shows Hulot following one
of the Dutch police officers across the police garage. The
officer holds his hands behind his head as he stretches his
tired neck. Walking past them from the opposite direction
is a cop marching behind a criminal whose hands are on
his head in the customary position of an arrested lawbreaker.
Suddenly it appears as if Hulot were leading the cop in front
of him away to jail. The funny situation is all pure coincidence and is all the funnier because no one involved in the
scene is even aware of what is happening.

Much of Tati's humor is based upon simple misunder-
standings. A fist fight between two motorists in Trafic is
neatly avoided when one of the antagonists, pulling off his
sweater, brushes his hair and mustache into a new style.
His angry opponent does not recognize the man and, unable
to find him, walks off angrily. The instance of Maria's
mistaking a sheepskin vest, crushed under the wheels of her
car, for her little dog is another, rather drawn-out, example.

Apart from the thought that goes into Tati's construction of filmic situations is Tati's physical ability as a performer. He has been able to integrate his ability in the
stylized art of pantomime with the more realistic require-
ments of film. His synthesis is Hulot. One sees within
Hulot not only pantomime, but acrobatic and gymnastic abilities, as well. Roger Manvell declared that the Hulot character

> shares a common inability to come to terms with
> the physical world, but gets in and out of difficult-
> ies with a balletic effrontery which turns his spe-
> cial awkwardness into an act of spirited grace.[156]

For such an experienced mime, Tati uses his face
very little, throwing the burden of self expression onto his
gangly limbed body. For this reason, Tati insists on using
wide shots which show the entire length of his body.

Simple exaggeration is Tati's final and most prevalent
comedy element. Hulot, similar to Harold Lloyd, is a character, who is more realistically drawn than many of the silent film clowns, and yet his personality is an amalgam of
exaggerations. He is over polite, over helpful, over curious,

As Monsieur Loyal, in his 1973 Swedish television production
Parade, Tati performs several of his earliest pantomimes,
including "The Horseman" and "The Tennis Player." (Courtesy Nicole Liss.)

over intimidated, over competitive and over detached. Tati's realistic settings are not exaggerations--they do exist
in this world, more and more so. However, Tati carefully chooses the most extreme examples of location or architecture that he can find. Playtime's bleak steel and glass
canyons are obvious forms of overstatement. Hulot's home
in the crumbling St. Maur district of Paris, together with
the Arpel's ultramodern home, are located at reality's opposite extremes. The endlessly busy highways and automobile dominated terrain of Trafic, despite their documentary
accuracy, seem almost to be an exaggeration due to the
omnipresence of the automobile. Although very few of Tati's players look any different from the average person on
the street, the pattern of their behavior is exaggerated.
The mindlessness with which they pursue their vacation activities, their tour of the city and all the other functions
society has laid out for them is, indeed, an exaggeration of
the actions of real people. In these very exaggerations
that which goes unnoticed in one's life is heightened to the
point of obviousness. One can see, perhaps for the first
time, the silliness of much that one takes seriously and the
importance of much that one disregards.

     None of these comedy elements or techniques are uni-
que unto Tati. They are used by any number of comedy
filmmakers. It is, however, the frequency and relentless-
ness with which Tati employs them, along with the awareness of where they can best be applied, that makes his use
of them something special. Tati's outlook on the world is
such that he observes, particularly, the truths that other
filmmakers ignore. Tati spends much of his time analyzing
these odd, incidental activities. When he shares his analy-
ses with his audience, via his use of the techniques discussed here, what results are Tati's eccentric and fascinating
comedies.

CHAPTER 14

THE TECHNICAL ASPECTS

In analyzing the technical aspects of Tati's films, one starts to realize that Tati's priorities are just about the reverse of other filmmakers. Film, being primarily a visual medium, is approached by most filmmakers with a concern and even a reverence for the image, for frame composition and for camera movement. Quite often the sound elements of a film are conceived of and applied only after the film is essentially complete. Tati, however, approaches sound as a very basic element, one that has endless potential. It is not merely something applied on top of an already finished work. However, Tati's use of the camera does seem to imply, at first glance, a lack of awareness of the visual potential. It seems as though Tati has approached the camera with as much naiveté as the early silent clowns did in their earliest films. Upon closer scrutiny however, one realizes that there is a strong conscious technique of camera work behind Tati's comedies.

Like Chaplin, Tati maintains a static camera. He sees no use for either tracking shots or pans because they neutralize whatever movement is taking place. The only time Tati's camera moves is when it simply readjusts the framing to follow the action within a scene. Tati's stage-oriented outlook is one of the main reasons for his disinclination toward an expressive use of the camera. Tati avoids close up shots, as well. In his democratic concept of comedy, he believes the audience should not be forced into watching only what the director wants them to watch. Tati prefers to have the audience sit back and choose whatever it wants to look at. Tati's training, as mentioned earlier, is designed toward the broad and full use of the body, much like Chaplin. His face will tell you much less than the attitude of his body. This style of performance requires wide-angle camera setups. In addition, a lot of the activity in

Tati's films is in a large scale--crowds of people, traffic
jams--all requiring that the camera be placed at a distance
away. Tati has stated:

> The dimension of the camera is the dimension of
> what your eyes see; I don't come close up or
> make tracking shots to show you what a good di-
> rector I am. I want your eye to put you in such
> a situation where <u>you</u> come to the opening of the
> restaurant as if you were there that night.[157]

Tati considers his use of the static long shot to be
a highly realistic use of the camera. It allows one, as a
spectator, to become more involved in the film. One
searches the horizon for François and his bicycle in <u>Jour
de Fête</u>, just as if one were a fellow villager anxiously a-
waiting the mail. Martine looking down upon the beach in
<u>Les Vacances</u>, the tourists staring up at the skyscrapers in
<u>Playtime</u> and the crowded auto show in <u>Trafic</u> are all pre-
sented from the point of view of a participant, of someone
actually involved in the story. Tati does not miraculously
zoom in for close-ups or rise high on a crane for an im-
personal bird's-eye view.

It seems only natural that Tati would progress to the
use of wide-screen techniques. He firmly believes that the
use of such film gauges as 70 millimeter should never have
been limited only to large-scale subject matter. <u>Playtime</u>,
Tati's first and only 70-millimeter production to date, is
aptly suited for the larger film size. The towering buildings
and crowds of people are particularly interesting subject matter in this new format. James Monaco has commented on
this:

> Tati, uniquely I believe, uses the wide film gauge
> not to provide extra area for a complicated mise-
> en-scène, but rather to emphasize in a surrealis-
> tic way the emptiness, the void of the clean glass
> city.[158]

Tati had considered color an important element in the
presentation of his films long before he ever got the opportunity to use it. As early as his first feature, <u>Jour de
Fête</u>, Tati was experimenting with a color process that failed. "To tell the truth," he has said, "even when I shot my
films in black and white, I always thought them in colour."[159]
The soft and warm pastels of the old St. Maur district in

Mon Oncle, juxtaposed with the cold and sterile greys and electric greens of the Arpel's household, are an excellent example of color as a thematic element, as are the greys, accompanied by other middle tones, that dominate Playtime. One can hardly imagine Tati's opposition of Old World versus New in Trafic without his having captured the incredibly lush coloring of the countryside that runs parallel to the highway. So intense was Tati's appreciation for the effect color can play in recounting his stories that he had, at some point before starting Playtime, dabbled in a process he called Scopochrome. Variety reported at the time:

> He says that he has latched onto a new process
> that can turn black and white pix into color opti-
> cally. Tati's idea is to release a flock of old
> slapstick and early silent U. S. comedies he has
> acquired as well as feature films turned into col-
> or by the process he has dubbed Scopochrome.[160]

One can only imagine what the final result of the process would have looked like. Although Tati even planned to tint his own early black-and-white films, he never followed through on the idea.

It is not unusual in a discussion of a filmmaker's technical standards to stop just short of any mention of the use of sound. In Tati's case a discussion could begin with his use of sound. According to Monaco, "Tati regards his sound tracks almost as separate films...."[161] Tati not only has his cast add in their lines of dialogue later in the ideal environment of the sound studio, but continues "writing" the film with the selection of sound effects for each of the visuals. Tati sees these postproduction activities in a unique light, one that accurately indicates his belief in the integrity of sound:

> It remains for me to 're-shoot' each scene, this
> time not for images but for sound. I take very
> great care with this aspect. Indeed I consider
> the sound to be of capital importance.[162]

Tati's "looping" of lines, that is to say his rerecording of actor's lines, in the studio, is not unusual in the film industry. However, Tati is one of the few directors who rerecords as a freely creative choice and not as a technique to salvage poorly recorded sequences. Not only does Tati realize the advantages of control that rerecording offers,

despite its difficulty, but like the silent clowns, he finds it
necessary to verbally coach his cast during actual shooting.
Rerecording, therefore, offers Tati full control during both
the shooting and the creation of the sound track.

Throughout Tati's works are examples of gags and
characters that rely, for the most part, upon the proper
selection of a sound effect: Hulot's backfiring little car, the
"plunk-plunk" of the dining room door and the garbled loudspeakers in the train station in Les Vacances as well as the
loud crunching of the maitre d's pepper mill in Playtime are all
Tati-esque sound gags at their finest. Tati foresees a time when
commercially accepted films will be made in which "you'll
have a very simple image with very little movement, and
the sound will add a new dimension, like putting sound in a
painting--whoosh."163

The state of silence allowed the silent clowns an unusual freedom. Being far removed from the natural state
of things, silent films could easily have characters pretend
to hear only those sounds that would heighten the effect intended by the scene. Tati claims this same freedom of
silence for himself in creating his universe. One can easily see Chaplin's approach to the natural world versus the
silent world, in Modern Times, as a model followed by Tati. Tati undermines some of the rigidity with which contemporary audiences approach a film. In so doing, he has freed
the audience from contemporary film's literal bonds and allowed them to partake of the freedom of expression and imagination that was thoughtlessly discarded at the advent of
sound.

Tati's inclination toward the use of wide screen, 70
millimeter has to do with his concern for sound quality as
much as it has to do with his ideas of visual composition.
This wider film gauge allows the use of stereophonic, magnetic sound tracks in place of the more conventional optical
sound tracks. Tati, it has been noted, withheld the American release of Playtime for some four years because of his
desire to have it shown only in theaters equipped to handle
it in its superior 70 millimeter version. He said:

> I've been fighting all my life for sound tracks.
> They're obliged to be magnetic one day; it's a
> joke for distributors to make them optical. With
> optical, beyond a certain point you get distortion,
> with magnetic you get all the range you want.164

It is not unusual for Tati to employ a particular
sound effect as a leitmotif, with a unifying effect, running
through his works. The comical sputtering of Hulot's car,
in Les Vacances, is heard at precisely the right moments.
One gets a sense of Hulot's relentless activity, always coming or going, as the sound of the backfiring car drifts
across a peaceful scene. The sounds of distant barking
dogs is used throughout a number of Tati's films. It is a
dog's far-off barking that heightens the precious calm after
Hulot has exploded a shack full of fireworks, in Les Vacances. Again, a dog's faint barking is heard, enhancing the
stillness of a few country scenes in Trafic.

After examining Tati's highly personal approach to
both sound and camera, it seems a bit anticlimatic to mention his editing style. From his earliest films, Tati has
shown little concern for editing as anything more than func-
tional. The expressive uses of pacing, intercutting and simple shot selection are only superficially employed by Tati.
He uses a wide-angle master shot to cover most scenes,
rather than cutting to a variety of different angles. In a
sense, Tati would like his audience to edit his sequences
for themselves, through their own perceptions. There may
be sequences and, more especially, certain gags that a
more conventional director would have been eager to edit
into a certain style. It can be seen as an example of Tati's simplicity and effectiveness that in his films they can
be played without the enhancement of anything but the simplest editorial technique.

Like all good filmmakers, Tati's approach to the
technical aspects of his films is done sensitively, with great
regard for the relationship of technique to content. The imprint of Tati's technical decisions adds character to his
comic universe almost as effectively as do his singular perceptions.

CHAPTER 15

MUSIC

     The music in Tati's films ranges from the gentle
chansons of Les Vacances to the spirited pop-jazz score of
Trafic. As Tati began more and more to clarify his opposing themes, he began, accordingly, to employ a broader
range of musical styles. The extremities of these styles
serve to focus attention upon a film's oppositions of new
versus old, efficient versus inefficient, sterility versus humanism. In all of Tati's films, the music imparts a light,
warm and gentle spirit which creates, in turn, a particularly French flavor.

     Alain Romans, the composer of the scores for Les
Vacances and Mon Oncle, believes Tati to have great taste
in his selection of music. Romans commented on the popularity of the music he composed for Tati's films:

          The themes are always a success in France but
          I'd like to add that Tati doesn't like to have any
          songs sung in his films. My themes become pop-
          ular songs a while after the films are released. [165]

Tati's integrity forces him to avoid the clever business ploys
that obtrusively interject potential hit songs into films where
they do not belong.

     Francis Lemarque, composer of the main themes in
Playtime, commented that

          Tati is an extremely sensitive artist, especially so
          with popular, unsophisticated music. When he
          loves a theme he will protect it with great loyalty
          and I would say with great tenderness. [166]

It is quite easy to see Tati's music hall background impress-

145

ing upon him the importance of music to comedy. He himself said:

> Music hall has taught me that it is often difficult
> to be funny without music, because being funny is
> like being on the highwire or juggling, so I try to
> have a tune in my head for actors.[167]

Tati often employs a number of composers in order to have
a wider selection of themes to choose from. Romans has
mentioned that Tati is "not able to suggest in detail what he
would like--when given a choice he can easily choose."[168]
Lemarque has recounted that he was selected to compose
the themes for Playtime only after Tati had proposed that a
number of composers work on developing a principal theme.
Lemarque explained that Tati

> waits until he is able to fall in love with one of
> them and that is how I ended up working on Play-
> time. I would add that to be sure he is not mak-
> ing a mistake Tati experiments with different rhy-
> thms and with varying the choice of instruments.[169]

Tati's typical perfectionism causes him to search thoroughly
for a musical style that he feels will best fit his film.
Frank Barcellini, Tati's composer for Mon Oncle, saw Tati's search for the proper musical treatment in this light:

> I think he's sensitive to the music just as one
> would be to a young girl, that is one is full of
> love one day and detests her the next.[170]

Jean Yatove, who composed the score not only for
Tati's first feature, Jour de Fête, but for two of his early
shorts, Soigne Ton Gauche and L'Ecole des Facteurs, admits
that working with Tati can be frustrating for a composer.
He finds that Tati's constant flexibility and experimentation
with the script causes difficulties in developing the final
themes. According to Yatove,

> Certain directors say, 'This theme I'll have re-
> corded so as to serve as a musical base or foun-
> dation for the filming of the scene.' Jacques Tati
> never does this. I will insist that he listen to cer-
> tain themes I've improvised for certain scenes but
> he doesn't want to hear them.[171]

Both Lemarque and Romans have mentioned that they only go so far as to compose the leitmotifs or themes for each character before the filming is completed. Tati never has music composed for the purpose of prepacing a particular scene. Romans said that Tati "especially insists that the music not underline the gestures or sound effects."172 One delightful exception to that is the synchronized highway line sequence from Trafic.

Corresponding to Tati's dislike for synchronizing music with visuals is his distaste for strong orchestration. The themes in his films are light and airy. The jazz themes that parallel the driving sequences in Trafic are arranged for a small combo. The film's harder rock themes, as well, are played by a small group. The lightly orchestrated music of Les Vacances is an especially good example of music enhancing the dreamy, lazy holiday mood of the film. Even when Tati unwisely insisted that Romans create a harsher, more up-to-date arrangement of the themes for the film's 1962 rerelease, he was still able to avoid an overbearing, full orchestration.

Throughout all the musical themes in Tati's films a strong sense of Tati's peculiarly satiric universe is reflected. Music of any other sensitivity could never have been integrated into Tati's vision. Not only is the music peculiarly French, but it is peculiarly suited to the character of Hulot as well. Charles Dumont's wide-ranging but simple score for Trafic keeps reverting back to his basic four note "da-da-dee-da" pattern. The constant recurrence of this pattern, no matter how deeply the themes may have moved into a jazz or rock style, is amusing in much the same way the constant reappearances of Hulot are amusing. The simple, unpretentious theme is as relentless and as powerful as the character of Hulot. Similar to Hulot, the theme lacks a certain substance or solidity which is well compensated for by its persistence. The older romantic themes, especially in Les Vacances and Mon Oncle, support and are, in turn, supported by the personality of Hulot. As one observes this comically out-of-place gentleman, the film's antique chansons seem suddenly in their proper place. The harder and jazzier themes, such as Mon Oncle's underscoring for the activities of the Arpels or David Stein's and James Campbell's increasingly intense music for the climactic Royal Garden sequence of Playtime, effectively add a feeling of coarseness and tension wherever introduced. Tati will very carefully reserve the softer sections of music

to accent precisely the right moments. A group of young
people, sitting by a riverside in Trafic, listen to the beautiful song one boy plays on his guitar. The scene is one
of a few preciously romantic moments in a film that is
otherwise dominated by the fast beat of the automobile and
its corresponding musical themes.

The music of Trafic in fact is perhaps the clearest
example of musical themes supporting opposing story elements in Tati's works. Dumont's score ranges from a soft-
ly romantic style to the harsh rock style of the film's traveling sequences. Tati goes a step further in this musical
treatment by allowing Dumont to incorporate some effective
expressive elements. A jazz-oriented drum solo accompan-
ies some of the more intense traveling scenes. Dumont
even blends in an agonized, wailing human voice to accompany, appropriately, a traffic jam sequence. But, like the
sweetly haunting theme of Les Vacances, the bouncy central
theme of Trafic reappears faithfully at the film's close.

Although he is not a musician, Tati insists on tight
control over his film's musical scores. If working relations
with some of his composers have become, at times, strained,
Tati's highly individual vision finds its way into the finished
scores nevertheless. Of the time he spent working with Tati on Playtime, Lemarque has said: "I better understand and
appreciate patience and the mastery of my nerves."173 If
Tati is going to go to all the trouble of writing, directing
and acting in his films, just so he may faithfully convey a
glimpse of the crazy world of his perceptions, then to allow
an element as infectious as music to be under another's control is to compromise that vision. Even though Tati's ideas
should perhaps at some points have benefitted from the scrutiny of his advisors or assistants, still they retain the agree-
able and unmistakable quality known to be his.

CHAPTER 16

CONCLUSION

No matter what words one may use in describing the
current cinema, one can always conclude by saying, "...
and, of course, there is also Jacques Tati." Although Tati's films have always resisted comparison to any of his
contemporaries', they are not islands separated from film
history. Perhaps, more than any other contemporary filmmaker, Tati has been influenced by the great silent clowns.
Combining elements of style and character, most obviously
from Linder, Chaplin, Keaton, Langdon and Lloyd, with his
own irreverant point of view on today's society, he has
created a distinctive comic universe. Tati is not, however,
a remnant of that early era of film. His works are not
nostalgic but vibrantly modern.

Tati has constantly turned the real world back upon
itself by reflecting society's behavior in the world he creates on the screen. Tati's purpose has been simply to
make people see their world with a new degree of objectivity and, in so doing, enable them to choose independently
how to lead their lives. Tati's films do succeed in opening
people's eyes, through outrageous comedy rather than
through propaganda.

Tati is the only current film clown to have created
an archetypal film character. In creating Hulot, Tati had
to free himself from relative or contemporary ideas of what
was funny and go back to a place of essential, fundamental
comedy inspiration, the place Chaplin's Tramp or Keaton's
Stoneface came from.

If Chaplin and the other great clowns had their flock
of imitators, one wonders why Tati remains virtually uncop-
ied in current cinema. As provocative as Tati's vision may

be, it may also be so individual as to discourage would-be imitators. The self-induced silence, for example, while it offers new freedom of expression, may be too great a barrier for current clowns to overcome. Relying solely upon one's physical abilities in order to get a laugh was something Tati, as a mime, was trained to do; few people working in film today have had such a background. Mel Brooks' Silent Movie, for example, is a rather pedestrian attempt at recapturing the special grace of silent comedies. For all its slapstick humor, it could not free itself from using funny title cards and succeeded more as a novelty than as a solidly engineered silent comedy.

It is a fairly straightforward process to trace influences upon Tati back through René Clair, Jean Renoir, Keaton, Chaplin and Linder. Looking for Tati's influence on current French cinema however is more difficult. His lighthearted optimism seems characteristic of most current French comedy. The Tall Blond Man with One Black Shoe and its sequels have successfully captured a slapstick style with their charmingly naive and long-legged main character, similar in stature and movements to Hulot. Rather than make fun of any social issues, the Tall Blond films simply satirize the secret agent film genre. Claude Lelouch's stylish comedies are very popular. His Money, Money, Money is a light slapstick spoof on bank robbers and the entire first reel of his Toute une Vie is a silent comedy sequence set to oldfashioned music. Truffaut's Small Change is a warmly funny view of childhood. The popular Cousin, Cousine gently and compassionately spoofs the accepted notions of marriage and fidelity. While these films are only a sampling of current French cinema, they do present a generally optimistic, non-judgmental view of life. Tati's films, unlike the early works that inspired them, and despite their satire, just as effectively avoid the bitterness and judgmental qualities that can rob a comedy of its power; one thinks, in example, of Chaplin's Monsieur Verdoux or the closing scene in his The Great Dictator. Just as the current French films demonstrate, Tati's comedy does not succeed by attacking or overpowering the audience, but by charming them.

In French comedies, as in current comedies elsewhere, the story remains the point of the film. With Tati the comedy is the point. He creates a universe in which something funny is always happening. The mood or environ-

ment in a Tati film is what keeps the audience interested
just as effectively as does the story in other films. Despite Tati's example, comedy still remains subordinate to
the story, appearing from moment to moment rather than
as a continuum as in Tati's films. One begins to sense
that Tati's vision and style are so much his own that few
other works will provide anything even close to what he
has to offer.

American producers have been interested in Tati because he is a truly international filmmaker. His films are
not essentially French any more than Chaplin's films were
strictly American. The Paris of Playtime is so frighten-
ingly real precisely because there is nothing Parisian about
it; it is an international city. Trafic, as well, could have
been filmed on any stretch of modern highway in the world.
It is ironic, therefore, that in the U.S. where the works of
Fellini, Truffaut and Bergman are so often seen, Tati's
first three features have not been screened, outside of rare
festival showings, for some years. With Tati's financial
difficulties following Playtime the distribution rights to his
films were thrown into legal question. Tati, himself, with-
drew Mon Oncle from distribution until the questions were
settled. Tati, who was never a prolific filmmaker, remains,
in this country, highly regarded, fondly remembered, but
rarely shown.

APPENDIX I

"CONFUSION"

Tati has, from time to time, toyed with the idea of
making a film in Hollywood. After Mon Oncle's smashing
success in America in 1958-59 the offers started to pour in
from the film capital. Hazel Flynn reported at the time:

> Nearly every studio in town has made the star-di-
> rector-writer-producer a fat offer. He can write
> his own ticket on most lots. But Tati has made
> it plain in a friendly way that while he would like
> to come here and work he doubted if the industry
> of today would approve his way of doing things. [174]

Tati was well aware that not even the most faithful and patient of Hollywood producers could suffer through his meticulous and time consuming approach to production. It was
not the first time that attempts had been made to lure him
from his personal style of film production. Sequels to Jour
de Fête had been eagerly proposed, with poor François having to get married or running off to Paris. Tati wisely declined these offers just as he declined an offer to make a
film in Italy with the famous clown Toto (Antonio de Curtis,
who died in 1967)--to be entitled, what else, Toto and Tati.
Flynn went on to describe Tati's reactions to the Hollywood
technique of film production:

> Apparently he aimed My Uncle at factory-made
> films (in his mind's eye) as well as appliances.
> 'Factory-made movies,' he declares, 'lead to de-
> cline. There must be originality, and this can
> not be achieved by using the same pattern over
> and over.' [175]

Tati has admitted he would like to make a film in

Hollywood, but was aware that few people would allow him the time he required. He cites the twenty-two week shooting schedule of Mon Oncle as an example. Harold Hildebrand reported, however, that "producers are eager to sign Tati on his own terms because they sense in him a new global star."[176] Although Tati wisely turned down such typical proposals as Mr. Hulot Goes West, one begins to wonder why, after all these years, Tati has never accepted an offer to come to the U.S. to make a film. To see Hollywood as the only center of filmmaking that has ever put profit before art is nonsense. Tati has resisted the very same profit motives in Europe for years. It would also seem that a Tati film made in America would have an instantaneously larger audience as a result of better distribution and promotion.

It appeared for a while in 1975 that Tati would, indeed, be coming to the U.S. to make his next film, entitled Confusion. The film, to have been financed by French and American sources and to have been produced by Robert Levinson and Steven North, was preciously close to getting under way when Tati decided to work with different producers and do the film in Europe, instead. Levinson's disappointment was evident:

> Tati, upon concluding a deal with us, bettered the deal with financial sources in three other countries. I suspect that he's both in awe of the concept of working in America, too timid to step away from the people and the technology he has worked with over the years and at this juncture in life more interested in protecting his secure reputation than in expanding his personal creative horizons.[177]

Confusion, as yet unmade, is to be structured on Tati's typical riffing style. Hulot would appear, here, as an ingenious inventor hired by an enterprising American television network to install his new Hulot-Color systems in their news camera. Traveling about with the television news crew gives Hulot ample opportunity to create his brand of havoc or, if you will, confusion in the most varied of locations.

Suffering all the electronic difficulties one would expect if Hulot came in contact with the complicated technology of television, he and his crew vainly attempt to keep up with the increasing flood of news. Tati has described one pro-

Tati in 1973 (courtesy Nicole Liss).

posed sequence, giving one a hint of the potential involved
in such a subject matter:

> Amidst the panic, Hulot's crew members have
> more and more technical difficulties, particularly
> with the sound track. As it is not correctly syn-
> chronized, musique, speeches, miaows, explosions
> and war effects all run together in a confused ca-
> cophony. [178]

Further experimenting with sound, Tati proposes to show
soldiers at rest, completely indifferent to the sounds of ma-
chine-gun fire and bombardment heard on the newsreel soundtrack. When the sounds suddenly change to birds chirping,
the soldiers react in fear as if they just heard the sounds of
attack.

The idea of Hulot-Color seems, itself, to be a paro-
dy of Tati's own experiments with different color processes.
In a comical ending, Tati proposes that Hulot's color system go completely awry as the crew films a military decor-
ation ceremony. The gold from the generals' caps starts
to run down their faces and the red from their numerous decorations starts to run down their uniforms like blood.

One can observe certain underlying themes working
their way into this proposal. The theme of man as a pawn
to his technology is evident here. People have become so
bored with their technology that it is necessary for television networks to present "special news" programs which are
more entertaining than straightforward news. One recalls
how the concept of the automobile was parodied by the
overcomplicated camping car in Trafic. This tendency to
complicate the technology would be clearly shown in Confusion, as well.

The woman character in Confusion would be a mem-
ber of the news crew and, like Maria, the freshly independent woman in Trafic, the woman would be, in Tati's own
words: "One of the very active members of the Hulot crew
... an authoritative woman of about forty with a Hulot-like
gait."[179] Again, Tati's efforts to establish that Hulot represents everybody, and vice versa, would be strengthened
by the woman's personality.

The news cameras capture many scenes in which
neither Hulot nor the crew takes part. In a scene that
would directly parallel some of Tati's ideas from Playtime,
one would watch a news report on tourism in France. The
cameras would catch a shot of a tourist bus as it approaches Paris. In Tati's own words:

> A new flow of tourists has come to Paris. We
> see loaded buses driving along the expressways
> then plunging down into the tunnels, causing pas-
> sengers to have but a flash vision of the reputed
> Parisian monuments.[180]

A scene showing a filmed report on a rowing competition along a beautiful river would rapidly reveal the clear
waters becoming polluted with trash and detergents. Trafic's
beautiful countryside, more and more cluttered with garbage
and discarded cars, is an earlier version of this kind of
scene. In Confusion Hulot's bosses grow increasingly angry

with the declining quality of the news reports. When the
confusion of mixed up sounds and images becomes too much
for Hulot and his crew, they simply walk away. In a way
similar to the ending of Trafic, Hulot is able to walk away
from the technology when those around him start to take it
too seriously. Hulot heads off down a deserted street and
"walks by a shop window where a television set has been
left on. A soundless speaker seems to reprimand the soli-
tary passerby who remains indifferent."[181] A dog then
crosses Hulot's path. Tati concluded his proposal with this
description:

> As night falls on the city, the roofs covered with
> television antennas give the impression that all the
> inhabitants are present in front of their television
> sets. Alone in the street, the dog goes off in the
> distance.[182]

The film would close on this note of indifference toward technology; the very same indifference that Hulot has exhibited
so effortlessly throughout a number of films.

Tati's use of the sound element would play a larger,
more direct part in this proposed project than in any of Tati's finished films. Tati would go so far as to rely upon
dialogue in certain scenes. When the television director accidentally sends the flowery and poetic opera reporter to
cover a sports event and the rather inarticulate sportscaster
ends up reporting the opera "in his habitual tone, with short
abrupt phrases,"[183] one realizes the new importance dialogue
would take in this film. Tati explains:

> The dialogue which, up until now, did not contri-
> bute to the plot of my films, will become indi-
> spensable, without however making the film too
> talky, which could be detrimental to the visual
> comic effects.[184]

Later in his proposal Tati goes on to explain that the
use of certain well-known actors would be considered if, indeed, the film were ever to be made in the U.S. Tati considers the use of stars in cameo roles as a concession to
having the film more widely distributed in this country. Tati also mentioned his willingness to collaborate with an American screenwriter for the purpose of facilitating the American public's comprehension of his style. These fundamental shifts in Tati's thinking may only be, in actuality, the

Tati in his Swedish television production, Parade (1973).
(Both courtesy Nicole Liss.)

kinds of things he finds necessary to say in order to reassure potential backers of his film's marketability. One suspects that the foreign backers who bettered the American deal with Tati will have to conform to Tati's independent style of production rather than the other way around.

Tati has not, however, been totally away from film production since the completion of Trafic. In 1973 he wrote, directed and starred in a feature-length film made for Swedish television, entitled Parade. An atypical fantasy, the film, which was actually done 70 percent in videotape, centers around the activity of a circus. Two small children are gradually brought closer together as they wend their separate ways through the activities of the circus. Tati appears as Monsieur Loyal, a circus performer, and performs some of his best-known pantomimes. Loyal is able to transform the mood of the circus into one of celebration and joy through the various music hall numbers he presents. The two children become friends at the close of the film. The circus tent is then seen standing empty in the windy night: a few stray balloons float past. One can see Tati's imprint upon the film in his celebration of the small children, in his portrayal of the tyranny of adults over children, in the comic vignettes of real people, and in his assembly of a large cast. The film is also Chaplinesque in ways that Tati's films with Hulot were not. Loyal is a less distracted, more down to earth character than Hulot. The film's sentimentality is also more obvious and, therefore, more Chaplinesque. The film was shown on French television on Christmas of 1973 and eventually won the French Grand Prix du Cinéma and the Gold Medal in the Children's Film Competition at the Moscow Film Festival in 1975. One only hopes that the film, like some of Bergman's television productions, finds its way to theatrical distribution.

FILMOGRAPHY

SHORT SUBJECTS

1932   Oscar, Champion de Tennis
Written by and starring Jacques Tati.

1934   On Demande une Brute
Written by Jacques Tati and Alfred Sauvy. Directed
by Charles Barrois. Assistant director: René Clément. Starring: Jacques Tati.

1935   Gai Dimanche
Written by Jacques Tati and the clown Rhum. Direct-
ed by Jacques Berr. Starring: Jacques Tati and
Rhum. Produced by Atlantic Films. 33 minutes.

1936   Soigne Ton Gauche
Written by Jacques Tati. Directed by René Clément.
Music by Jean Yatove. Starring: Jacques Tati. Pro-
duced by Cady Films (Fred Orain). 20 minutes.

1938   Retour à la Terre
Written by and starring Jacques Tati.

1947   L'Ecole des Facteurs
Written and directed by and starring Jacques Tati.
Assistant director: Henri Marquet. Camera: Louis
Félix. Music: Jean Yatove. Produced by Cady Films
(Fred Orain). 18 minutes. (Winner of the Max Lin-
der Award for Best Short Comedy, 1949.)

FEATURE LENGTH FILMS

1945   Sylvie et le Fantôme
Director: Claude Autant-Lara. Tati in role of ghost.

1946 **Le Diable au Corps**
Directed by Claude Autant-Lara. Tati in the role of
one of a group of soldiers: additional scenes in which
he appeared were cut.

1949 **Jour de Fête**
Written by Jacques Tati, Henri Marquet and René
Wheeler. Directed by Jacques Tati. Set design:
René Moulaert. Camera: Jacques Mercanton and
Marcel Franchi. Music: Jean Yatove. Editor: Mar-
cel Moreau. Produced by Cady Films (Fred Orain).
English version prepared by Borrah Minnevitch and
released by Arthur Mayer and Edward Kingsley.
Starring: Jacques Tati (François the Postman), Guy
Decomble (Roger, the circus owner), Paul Frankeur
(Marcel, a circus assistant), Santa Relli (an old lady,
Roger's wife), Maine Vallee (Jeannette, the young
girl), Roger Rafal (the barber), Beauvais (the café
owner), Delcassan (the cinema operator) and the inha-
bitants of Sainte-Sévère-sur-Indre.
Winner of the prize for the Best Scenario at the Ven-
ice Film Festival, 1949 and the French Grand Prix du
Cinéma, 1950.

1953 **Les Vacances de Monsieur Hulot**
Written by Jacques Tati and Henri Marquet with the
collaboration of P. Aubert and J. Lagrange. Direct-
ed by Jacques Tati. Set design: R. Briancourt and
H. Schmitt. Camera: Jacques Mercanton and Jean
Mousselle. Music: Alain Romans. Editors: Baron,
Bretoneiche and Grassi. Artistic consultant: Henri
Marquet. Produced by Cady Films (Fred Orain) and
Discina et Éclair Journal.
Starring: Jacques Tati (M. Hulot), Nathalie Pascaud
(Martine), Louis Perrault (Fred), Michèle Rolla (Mar-
tine's aunt), André Dubois (the commandant), Suzy
Willy (the commandant's wife), Valentine Camax (the
Englishwoman), Lucien Frégis (the hotel keeper),
Marguerite Gérard (the strolling woman), René La-
court (the strolling man), Raymond Carl (the boy),
Michèle Brabo (a woman vacationer), Georges Adlin
(the South American).
Winner of International Critics Prize at the Cannes
Film Festival, 1953, the Femina Prize and the Louis
Delluc Award, 1953.

1958   Mon Oncle
        Written by Jacques Tati with the collaboration of
        Jacques Lagrange and Jean L'Hote. Directed by
        Jacques Tati. Set design: Henri Schmitt. Camera:
        Jean Bourgoin. Assistant directors: Henri Marquet
        and Pierre Etaix. Music: Frank Barcellini and
        Alain Romans. Sound: Jacques Carrère. Editor:
        Suzanne Baron. Production manager: Bernard Maur-
        ice. Produced by Fred Orain, Specta Films, Gray
        Film, Alter Films (Paris). Associate producers: L.
        Dolivet and A. Térouanne. Studios: Nice (La Victo-
        rine). Exteriors: Créteil and Saint-Maur-des-Fossés.
            Starring: Jacques Tati (M. Hulot), Jean-Pierre Zola
        (M. Arpel), Adrienne Servantie (Mme. Arpel), Alain
        Bécourt (Gérard), Lucien Frégis (Pichard), Domini-
        que Marie (the neighbor woman), Betty Schneider
        (the landlord's daughter), J. F. Martial (Walter),
        André Dino (the sweeper), Max Martel (the drunkard),
        Yvonne Arnaud (the Arpel's maid), Claude Badolle
        (the junkman), Nicolas Bataille (the workman), Régis
        Fontenay (the suspenders salesman), Adélaide Daniel-
        li (Mme. Pichard), Denise Péronne (Mlle. Février),
        Michel Goyot (the auto salesman), Francomme (the
        painter), Dominique Derly (M. Arpel's secretary),
        Claire Rocca (Mme. Arpel's friend), Jean Rémoleux
        (the client in the factory), Mancini (the Italian mer-
        chant), René Lord, Nicole Regnault, Jean Meyet, Su-
        zanne Franck, Loriot and the inhabitants of the old
        Saint-Maur district of Paris.
            Winner of the Special Jury Prize at the Cannes Film
        Festival, 1958, the New York Film Critic's Award,
        1959 and the Academy Award for the Best Foreign
        Film of the Year, 1959.

1967   Playtime
        Written and directed by Jacques Tati. Artistic col-
        laboration: Jacques Lagrange. English dialogue: Art
        Buchwald. Architect-Set designer: Eugène Roman.
        Camera: Jean Badal and Andreas Winding (camera
        operators: Paul Rodier and Marcel Franchi). Music:
        Francis Lemarque ("Take My Band" by David Stein,
        African themes by James Campbell). Sound: Jacques
        Maumont. Editor: Gérard Pollicand. Production
        manager: Bernard Maurice. Produced by Specta
        Films. Associate producer: René Silvera.
            Starring: Jacques Tati (M. Hulot) and, in order of
        appearance, the female characters: Barbara Dennek

(the young tourist), Jacqueline Lecomte (her friend),
Valérie Camille (M. Lucs' secretary), France Rumil-
ly (woman selling the eyeglasses), France Delahalle
(shopper in the department store), Laure Paillette
and Colette Proust (the two women at the lamp), Eri-
ka Dentzler (Mme. Giffard), Yvette Ducreux (the hat
check girl), Rita Maiden (Mr. Schultz's companion),
Nicole Ray (the singer), Luce Bonifassy, Evy Caval-
laro, Alice Field, Eliane Firmin-Didot, Ketty France,
Nathalie Jam, Oliva Poli, Sophie Wennek.

The male characters: Jack Gauthier (the guide), Hen-
ri Piccoli (an important gentleman), Léon Doyen (the
doorman), Georges Montant (M. Giffard), John Abbey
(Mr. Lucs), Reinhart Kolldehoff (the German business-
man), Grégory Katz (the German salesman), Marc
Monjou (the false Hulot), Yves Barsacq (the friend),
Tony Andal (the page boy at the Royal Garden), André
Fouché (the manager), Georges Faye (the architect),
Michel Fancini (the first maitre d'), Billy Kearns
(Mr. Schultz), Bob Harley, Jacques Chauveau, Doug-
las Reard (guests at the Royal Garden), François
Viaur (the unlucky waiter), Gilbert Reeb (another
waiter), Billy Bourbon (the bartender).

Winner of Grand Prix de l'Académie du Cinéma, E-
toile de Cristal, 1968, Danish Academy Award for
the Best European Film of the Year, 1969, and the
Prix d'Argent at the Moscow Film Festival, 1969.

1971   Trafic
Written by Jacques Tati with the collaboration of Jac-
ques Lagrange. Directed by Jacques Tati. Set de-
sign: Adrien de Rooy. Music: Charles Dumont. Ca-
mera: Andreas Winding. Produced by Robert Dorf-
mann, Films Corona (Paris), Gibé Films and Oceania
Films (Rome). Released in the U.S. by Columbia
Pictures.
Starring: Jacques Tati (M. Hulot), Maria Kimberly
(Maria), Marcel Fraval (Marcel, the truck driver),
Honoré Bostel, François Maisongrosse, Tony Knep-
pers.

1973   Parade
Written and directed by Jacques Tati. Assistant di-
rector: Marie-France Siegler. Camera: Jean Badal
and Yunnar Fisher (camera operators: René Chabal,
Jens Fisher, Bengt Nordwall). Sound: Jean Neny.
Editors: Sophie Tatischeff, Per Carlesson, Siv Lund-

gren, Jonny Mair and Aline Fress. Artistic consul-
tant: François Bronett. Music: Charles Dumont.
Music arranged by: Armand Migiani ("Tax Free" by
Jan Carlsson). Publicity graphics: Jacques Lagrange.
Produced by Gray Film, Sveriges Radio and CEPEC.
Producers: Louis Dolivet, Michel Chauvin. Execu-
tive producer: Karl Haskel.

Starring: Jacques Tati (M. Loyal), Karl Kossmayer
and his mule, the Williams, the Vétérans, the Sipo-
loes, Pierre Bramma, Michèle Brabo, Pia Colombo,
Hall, Norman and Ladd, Les Argentinos, Johnny
Lonn, Bertilo, Jan Swahn, Bertil Berglund, Moniqa
Sunnerberg.

Winner of the Gold Medal in the children's film competition at the Moscow Film Festival, 1975.

CHAPTER NOTES

CHAPTER 1

1. "Interview with Tati," Les Nouvelles Littéraires, December 28, 1967.
2. Stanley Kauffmann, New Republic, July 21, 1973, p. 24.
3. Basil Wright, The Long View (New York: Knopf, 1974), p. 263.
4. Penelope Houston, "Conscience and Comedy," Sight and Sound, summer-autumn 1959, p. 161.
5. Hazel Flynn, Beverly Hills Citizen, January 28, 1959.

CHAPTER 2

6. Georges Sadoul, French Film (London: Falcon Press, 1953), p. 12.
7. Sadoul, op. cit., p. 13.
8. Armand J. Cauliez, Jacques Tati (Paris: Editions Seghers, 1968), p. 35.
9. Basil Wright, The Long View (New York: Knopf, 1974), p. 263.
10. Walter Kerr, The Silent Clowns (New York: Knopf, 1975), p. 78.
11. Cauliez, op. cit., p. 19.
12. Gerald Mast, The Comic Mind (New York: Bobbs-Merrill, 1973), p. 293.
13. Kerr, op. cit., p. 118.
14. Ibid., p. 117.
15. Philip Strick, Films and Filming, May 1962, p. 51.
16. Kerr, op. cit., p. 265.
17. Ibid., p. 268.
18. Ibid., p. 48.

CHAPTER 3

19. Penelope Gilliatt, New Yorker, August 28, 1971.

20. Kevin Thomas, "Jacques Tati: Silent Comedy Heir,"
Los Angeles Times, November 24, 1972.
     21. Colette, Le Journal, July 1936.
     22. Thomas, op. cit.
     23. Armand J. Cauliez, Jacques Tati (Paris: Editions
Seghers, 1968), p. 11.
     24. Georges Sadoul, The French Film (London: Falcon
Press, 1953), p. 63.
     25. Roy Armes, French Film (New York: Dutton,
1970), p. 35.
     26. Arthur Knight, The Liveliest Art, (New York:
Mentor Books, New American Library, 1957), pp. 154-55.
     27. Cauliez, op. cit., p. 36.
     28. Claude Beylie, "Tati inconnu," Cinéma 57, no. 23
(Noël, 1957), quoted in Philip Strick, Films and Filming,
May 1962, p. 49.
     29. Philip Strick, Films and Filming, May 1962,
p. 49.
     30. Ibid., p. 49.
     31. Claude Beylie, quoted in Cauliez, Jacques Tati,
pp. 150-51.
     32. Ibid., p. 150.
     33. Ibid., pp. 151-52.
     34. Ibid., p. 152.
     35. Ibid.

CHAPTER 4

     36. New York Times, February 20, 1952.
     37. Ibid.
     38. News Chronicle, quoted in Strick, p. 53.
     39. London Daily Mail quoted in Strick, p. 53.
     40. Georges Sadoul, French Film (London: Falcon
Press, 1953), p. 123.
     41. Time, March 31, 1952, p. 102.
     42. Philip Strick, Films and Filming, May 1962, p. 53.
     43. Dilys Powell, Sunday Times (London), February 20,
1952.
     44. Strick, op. cit., p. 53.
     45. Ibid.
     46. C. A. Lejeune, quoted in Strick, p. 53.
     47. Matthew Norgate, quoted in Strick, p. 53.
     48. Sadoul, op. cit., p. 119.
     49. Ibid., p. 121.
     50. New York Times, February 20, 1952.
     51. Roy Armes, French Cinema Since 1946, vol. I, The
Great Tradition (Cranbury, N. J.: A. S. Barnes, 1966, 1970).

CHAPTER 5

52.   Philip Strick, Films and Filming, May 1962, p. 51.
53.   Walter Kerr, The Silent Clowns, (New York: Knopf, 1975).
54.   Jacques Tati, quoted in Penelope Gilliatt, New Yorker, January 27, 1973, p. 40.
55.   Tati, quoted in Armand J. Cauliez, Jacques Tati (Paris: Editions Seghers, 1968), p. 9.
56.   Philip Strick, Films and Filming, May 1962, p. 51.
57.   Penelope Gilliatt, New Yorker, August 28, 1971.
58.   Roy Armes, French Cinema Since 1946, vol. I, The Great Tradition (Cranbury, N. J.: A. S. Barnes, 1966, 1970).
59.   Tati, quoted in Mary Blume, Los Angeles Times, September 6, 1970.
60.   Gerald Mast, The Comic Mind (New York: Bobbs-Merrill, 1973), p. 295.
61.   Tati, quoted in Films and Filming, August 1957, p. 15.
62.   Tati, quoted ibid.
63.   André Bazin, Qu'est-ce-que le Cinéma?, vol. I (Paris: Editions du Cerf., 1958).
64.   Ibid.
65.   Gilliatt, New Yorker, August 28, 1971.

CHAPTER 6

66.   Arthur Knight, Saturday Review, June 19, 1954.
67.   Jacques Tati, quoted in Edwin Schallert, "Even Other Comics Ask, 'Who's Tati?,'" Los Angeles Times, March 13, 1955.
68.   Knight, op. cit.
69.   Newsweek, June 21, 1954, p. 86.
70.   Janet Flanner (as Génet), The New Yorker, September 12, 1953.
71.   Tati, quoted in Schallert, op. cit.
72.   Letter to author from Alain Romans, Paris, February 23, 1976.
73.   Flanner, op. cit.

CHAPTER 7

74.   Armand J. Cauliez, Jacques Tati (Paris: Éditions Seghers, 1968), p. 49.

75. Jacques Tati, quoted ibid., p. 10.
76. Philip Strick, Films and Filming, May 1962,
p. 53.
77. Cauliez, op. cit., p. 30.
78. Penelope Gilliatt, The New Yorker, August 28,
1971.
79. Cauliez, op. cit., p. 41.
80. Gilliatt, op. cit.
81. Penelope Houston, "Conscience and Comedy,"
Sight and Sound, summer-autumn 1959, p. 162.
82. Ibid.
83. Tati, quoted in Strick, p. 51.
84. Houston, op. cit., p. 162.
85. Pierre Marcabru, "Jacques Tati contre l'ironie
française," Arts, March 8, 1961.
86. Arthur Knight, The Liveliest Art (New York: New
American Library, 1957), p. 193.

CHAPTER 8

87. Daily Variety, April 6, 1959.
88. Weekly Variety, November 6, 1963.
89. A. H. Weiler, New York Times, January 10, 1965.
90. Jacques Tati, quoted in Hazel Flynn, Beverly Hills
Citizen, January 28, 1959.
91. Armand J. Cauliez, Jacques Tati (Paris: Éditions
Seghers, 1968), p. 71.
92. Cauliez, op. cit., p. 18.
93. Cauliez, op. cit., p. 68
94. Walter Kerr, The Silent Clowns (New York: Knopf,
1975), p. 250.
95. Tati, quoted in Jonathan Rosenbaum, Film Comment,
May-June 1973, p. 40.
96. R. C. Dale, Film Quarterly, No. 2 (1972-73),
p. 31.
97. Jonathan Rosenbaum, Film Comment, May-June
1973, p. 37.
98. Ibid.
99. Tati, quoted in Rosenbaum, p. 39.
100. Rosenbaum, op. cit., p. 37.
101. Roy Armes, French Cinema Since 1946, vol. I,
The Great Tradition (Cranbury, N. J.: A. S. Barnes, 1966,
1970) p. 151.
102. Jean L'Hote, Cinéma 56, No. 19.
103. Tati, quoted in Armes, French Cinema, vol. I,
p. 151.

104. Cauliez, op. cit., p. 71.
105. Mary Blume, Los Angeles Times, September 6, 1970.
106. Ibid.
107. James Monaco, Take One, vol. 3, no. 11 (September 1972), p. 40.
108. Stanley Kauffmann, New Republic, July 21, 1973, p. 24.
109. Penelope Gilliatt, New Yorker, January 27, 1973, p. 42.
110. Kauffmann, op. cit., p. 24.
111. Rosenbaum, op. cit., p. 41.
112. Ibid.
113. Cauliez, op. cit., p. 75.
114. Tati, quoted in Rosenbaum, p. 34.
115. Tati, quoted ibid., p. 40.
116. Monaco, op. cit., p. 41.
117. Kauffmann, op. cit., p. 29.
118. Cauliez, op. cit., p. 74.
119. Dale, op. cit., p. 31.
120. Tati, quoted in Cauliez, p. 73.
121. Tati, quoted ibid.
122. Rosenbaum, op. cit., p. 36.
123. Tati, quoted in Rosenbaum, p. 40.
124. Rosenbaum, op. cit., p. 36.
125. Tati, quoted in Rosenbaum, p. 40.
126. Dale, op. cit., p. 31.
127. Tati, quoted in Rosenbaum, p. 41.

CHAPTER 9

128. Jacques Tati, quoted in Jonathan Rosenbaum, Film Comment, May-June 1973, p. 39.
129. James Monaco, Take One, vol. 3, no. 11 (September 1973), p. 40.
130. Roy Armes, French Film (New York: Dutton, 1970), p. 84.
131. Monaco, op. cit., p. 43.
132. Ibid., p. 40.
133. R. C. Dale, Film Quarterly, no. 2 (1972-73), p. 31.

CHAPTER 10

134. Penelope Gilliatt, The New Yorker, August 28, 1971.

135. R. C. Dale, Film Quarterly, no. 2, (1972-73), p. 31.
136. Jacques Tati, quoted in Jonathan Rosenbaum, Film Comment, May-June 1973, p. 40.
137. Tati, quoted ibid., p. 41.
138. Tati, quoted in Penelope Gilliatt, The New Yorker, January 27, 1973, p. 41.
139. Tati, quoted in Mary Blume, Los Angeles Times, September 6, 1970.

CHAPTER 11

140. Penelope Gilliatt, The New Yorker, August 28, 1971.
141. R. C. Dale, Film Quarterly, no. 2 (1972-73), p. 31.
142. Gilliatt, op. cit.

CHAPTER 12

143. André Bazin, Qu'est-ce-que le Cinéma?, vol. I, (Paris: Editions du Cerf, 1958).
144. Jonathan Rosenbaum, Film Comment, May-June 1973, p. 36.
145. Basil Wright, The Long View (New York: Knopf, 1974), p. 264.
146. Jacques Tati, quoted in Jonathan Rosenbaum, Film Comment, May-June 1973, p. 41.
147. Roy Armes, French Film (New York: Dutton, 1970), p. 85.
148. Tati, quoted in Rosenbaum, p. 40.

CHAPTER 13

149. Armand J. Cauliez, Jacques Tati (Paris: Editions Seghers, 1968), p. 39.
150. Walter Kerr, The Silent Clowns (New York: Knopf, 1975).
151. Gerald Mast, The Comic Mind (New York: Bobbs-Merrill, 1973), p. 7
152. Cauliez, op. cit., p. 32.
153. Stanley Kauffmann, The New Republic, July 21, 1973, p. 24.
154. Roy Armes, French Cinema Since 1946, vol. I,

The Great Tradition (Cranbury, N. J.: A. S. Barnes, 1966, 1970), p. 155.

155. Penelope Gilliatt, The New Yorker, (August 28, 1971).

156. Roger Manville, New Cinema in Europe (New York: Dutton, 1966), pp. 92-93.

CHAPTER 14

157. Jacques Tati, quoted in Jonathan Rosenbaum, Film Comment, May-June 1973, p. 39.

158. James Monaco, Take One, vol. III, no. 11 (September 1973), p. 41.

159. Tati, quoted in Roy Armes, French Cinema Since 1946, vol. I, The Great Tradition (Cranbury, N. J.: A. S. Barnes, 1966, 1970), p. 155.

160. Weekly Variety, November 6, 1963.

161. Monaco, op. cit., p. 41.

162. Tati, quoted in Armes, vol. I, p. 153.

163. Tati, quoted in Rosenbaum, p. 39.

164. Tati, quoted ibid.

CHAPTER 15

165. Letter to author from Alain Romans, Paris, February 23, 1976.

166. Letter to author from Francis Lemarque, La Varenne-St.-Maur, France, February 24, 1976.

167. Jacques Tati, quoted in Penelope Gilliatt, The New Yorker, January 27, 1973.

168. Letter from Romans.

169. Letter from Lemarque.

170. Letter to author from Frank Barcellini, Paris, March 17, 1976.

171. Letter to author from Jean Yatove, St. Cloud, France, February 21, 1976.

172. Letter from Romans.

173. Letter from Lemarque.

APPENDIX I

174. Hazel Flynn, Beverly Hills Citizen, January 28, 1959.

175. Ibid.

176. Harold Hildebrand, Los Angeles Examiner, January 18, 1959.

177. Letter to author from Robert Levinson, Hollywood, Calif., October 28, 1975.

178. Jacques Tati, Film Treatment for Confusion, April 1975.

179. Ibid.

180. Ibid.

181. Ibid.

182. Ibid.

183. Ibid.

184. Ibid.

BIBLIOGRAPHY

BOOKS

Armes, Roy. French Cinema Since 1946. Vol. I: The
Great Tradition. Cranbury, N. J.: A. S.
Barnes and Co., 1966, 1970.

_____. French Film. New York: E. P. Dutton and
Co., 1970.

Bazin, André. Collection "7e Art." Vol. I: Qu'est ce-que
le cinéma? Paris: Editions du Cerf, 1958.

Cauliez, Armand J. Jacques Tati. Paris: Editions Seghers, 1968.

Kerr, Walter. The Silent Clowns. New York: Alfred A.
Knopf, 1975.

Manville, Roger. New Cinema in Europe. New York:
E. P. Dutton and Co., 1966.

Mast, Gerald. The Comic Mind. New York: Bobbs-Merrill, 1973.

Sadoul, Georges. The French Film. London: The Falcon
Press, 1953.

Wright, Basil. The Long View. New York: Alfred A.
Knopf, 1974.

ARTICLES

Blume, Mary. "Tati Back in Comic Mood for Latest Hulot
Film," Los Angeles Times, Sept. 6, 1970.

Dale, R. C. "Playtime and Traffic, Two New Tati's,"
Film Quarterly, No. 2 (1972-73), p. 31.

Flanner, Janet. "Letter from Paris," by Genet [pseud.],
    The New Yorker, Sept. 12, 1953.

Flynn, Hazel. Beverly Hills Citizen, Jan. 28, 1959.

"French Comedy Writer Sees Tele Making All Future Pix
    Big Scale," Weekly Variety, November 6, 1963.

Gilliatt, Penelope. "The Current Cinema," New Yorker,
    August, 28, 1971.

_____. "Profiles," The New Yorker, Jan. 27, 1973.

Hildebrand, Harold. "U. S. Films May Acquire a New Di-
    mension: Tati," Los Angeles Examiner, Jan. 18,
    1959.

Houston, Penelope. "Conscience and Comedy," Sight and
    Sound, summer-autumn 1959, p. 161.

"Imports," Time, March 31, 1952, p. 102.

Kauffmann, Stanley. "Stanley Kauffmann on Films," New
    Republic, July 21, 1973, p. 24.

Knight, Arthur. "One Man's Movie," Saturday Review,
    June 19, 1954.

L'Hote, Jean. Cinema 56, No. 19, n.d.

"Make Them Laugh," Films and Filming, August 1957,
    p. 15.

Marcabru, Pierre. "Jacques Tati contre l'ironie fran-
    çaise," Arts, March 8, 1961.

Monaco, James. "Oldies But Goodies, Materialist Farce:
    Jacques Tati's 'Traffic' and 'Playtime'," Take One,
    III, no. 11 (September 1972), p. 40.

"New Films," Newsweek, June 21, 1954, p. 86.

Powell, Dilys. "A Laugh at Last," Sunday Times (London),
    Feb. 20, 1952.

Rosenbaum, Jonathan. "Tati's Democracy," Film Comment,
    May-June 1973, pp. 36-41.

Schallert, Edwin. "Even Other Comics Ask, 'Who's Tati?'," Los Angeles Times, March 13, 1955.

Strick, Philip. "Jour de Fête," Films and Filming, May 1962, p. 51.

"Tati (Hulot) Wants to Make Films Here, But with Control," Daily Variety, April 6, 1959.

Thomas, Kevin. "Jacques Tati: Silent Comedy's Heir," Los Angeles Times, November 24, 1972.

Weiler, A. H. New York Times, February 20, 1952.

_____. "It's Tati Time in Paris," New York Times, Jan. 10, 1965.

UNPUBLISHED MATERIAL

Letter from Frank Barcellini (Composer, Mon Oncle, score) Paris, March 17, 1976.

Letter from Francis Lemarque, (Composer, Playtime, score) La Varenne-St.-Maur, France, February 24, 1976.

Letter from Robert Levinson (Producer), Hollywood, Calif. October, 28, 1975.

Letter from Alain Romans (Composer, Les Vacances de Monsieur Hulot and Mon Oncle, scores), Paris, February 23, 1976.

Letter from Jean Yatove (Composer, Jour de Fête, score), St. Cloud, France, February 21, 1976.

Tati, Jacques. "Confusion," Proposal for film, April 1975.

INDEX